Forty Days Alone in Thailand

Jesus, the Buddha, Thai Culture and My Self

By

Tom Holmes

Forty Days Alone in Thailand
by Tom Holmes,
© by Tom Holmes, 2014

Published by
Chauncey Park Press
735 N. Grove Avenue
Oak Park, Illinois 60302
chauncey@wells1.com

Printed in the United States of America
Library of Congress: TXU001897346
ISBN: 978-1500622053

Dedicated to:

Sanit and Jiraporn Katika

I hope that travelling along with me in Thailand will encourage you on your walk through life.

Tom Holmes

TABLE OF CONTENTS

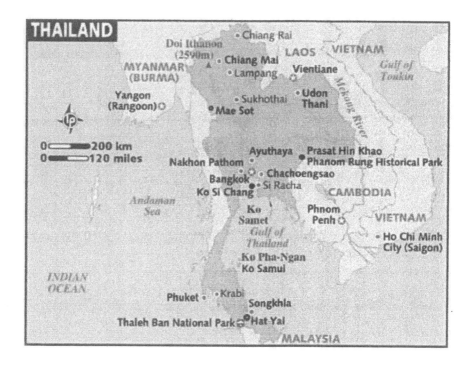

INTRODUCTION

A few years ago I wrote a column for the local newspaper with the headline *If You're Comfortable, It's Not Multicultural.*
The piece grew out of my 25 years of experience as the pastor of a congregation near Chicago which was 25% African American, 10% Hispanic and 65% Caucasian. On top of that we shared our building with a partner congregation, The Thai Community Church.

I would explain the challenge of my job by saying, "In a homogeneous congregation or community, members identify a problem and then debate the solution. In a multicultural situation, stake holders begin by debating the nature of the problem." That's because different cultures view what they see through different interpretive lenses. Sometimes the multicultural encounters result in unexpected gifts of grace and sometimes in discouraging frustration.

In 2009, I realized that I had forty days of unscheduled time in Thailand between the seventh mission trip I had helped lead in the "Land of Smiles" and an international conference in Pattaya on the Gulf of Thailand. I was at a point in my life where I felt the need to test my two primary relationships: with God and with my self.

Thai culture in general and Buddhism in particular, to me, would provide what Richard Rohr refers to as "a wall to butt up against. . .a worthy opponent against which we test our mettle." "Wholeness and holiness," he declared, "will always stretch us beyond our small comfort zone." The Gospel of Matthew states that it was the Spirit that led Jesus into the wilderness to be tested by the devil. Thai culture and Buddhism certainly aren't the devil incarnate. It was the testing part of the story which was pushing me.

I grabbed the opportunity to test these two relationships by traveling around Thailand alone—with my limited Thai vocabulary and my neurological disorder--to plunge into the deep end of the cultural pool, if you will, and see if I would sink or swim. Before leaving I joked with my friends and family that my only traveling companions would be my self and God, and I didn't know if I would get along with either one.

I wrote *Forty Days Alone in Thailand* partly as a spiritual travel memoir, but partly as a way of encouraging readers to risk moving out of their cultural comfort zones as a way of meeting themselves again as if for the first time.

Bill Bishop, in *The Big Sort, Why the Clustering of Like-Minded America is Tearing Us Apart*, writes, "As Americans have moved over the past three decades, they have clustered in communities of sameness, among people with similar ways of life, beliefs, and, in the end, politics."

"And we are living with the consequences of this segregation by way of life," he argues, "pockets of like-minded citizens that have become so ideologically inbred that we don't know, can't understand, and can barely conceive of 'those people' who live just a few miles away."

I hope and pray that the vicarious trip through Thailand this memoir provides will expose readers to the values, customs and ways of life of one segment of "those people" which will help them see themselves, their faith and their culture in new ways.

1

Bikkhu Buddha Dhatu

I had gotten on the train in Aranya on the Cambodian border at 6:30 in the morning, and had three hours to kill in Bangkok's cavernous Hualamphong Station before boarding the overnight train to Chiang Mai at 6:30 pm.

After snacking on two Chinese buns filled with pork and an iced coffee, I set out to explore the shops surrounding the main floor. When I got to the section reserved for Buddhist monks, which all airports and train stations in Thailand provide, I saw ten monks dressed in saffron and orange sitting together.

"This is a good picture," I thought, so I held up my camera to a monk sitting in the first row. When he gave me a slight nod, I focused the camera and took the picture. As I made a *wai* with my hands together in a prayer-like gesture to thank him, the monk patted the empty seat next to him.

"You mean me?" I indicated by pointing to myself.

Again a slight nod.

I didn't think this sort of thing was permitted, a layperson much less a *farang*, a Westerner, sitting with the monks. He nodded and patted the empty seat again.

I couldn't believe my good fortune. I love this sort of thing, crossing cultural and religious boundaries, connecting with people who think and believe differently than I do. One of my part time jobs back in the States is writing on religion for the local newspaper, a job in which I've interviewed everything from secular Jews to army chaplains to Buddhist teachers to Baha'is to gay pastors.

At the same time I felt anxiety about violating a cultural taboo regarding how lay people should relate to monks. I didn't think lay folk were even allowed to sit in the monks' section, yet this monk had invited me, so this white guy with a beard dressed in a polo shirt and khaki pants joined the group of self-contained men with shaved heads.

Bikkhu Buddha Dhatu (on the right)

In excellent English, he asked me my name and where I was from—standard questions Thais ask *farang*. I went along with the small talk for a minute, but decided I would shift the conversation to what I was really interested in, i.e. getting a deeper understanding of what serious Buddhists really think and feel.

"Would you teach me about Buddhism?" I asked, hoping he was willing to have an exchange on that level. "I know a little bit about

Buddhism, like the Four Noble Truths and the Eightfold Path, but I'd like to learn more. What would you say are the main differences between Buddhism and Christianity?"

Without hesitation he replied, "No difference." He rummaged in his bag and pulled out a book entitled *The Truth Of The Messengers, Questions and Answers With Bikkhu Buddha Dhatu, Beggar Of The Century.* He turned to the back of the book where three passages from the New Testament were printed as evidence that Buddhism and Christianity were compatible, and he repeated, "No difference."

I had heard "no difference" several times before from Buddhists like Thich Nhat Hanh (*Living Buddha, Living Christ*). *Pluralists* are what scholars call them, i.e. people who contend that all religions are the same at their core. Even the Dalai Lama sounds like a pluralist at times. Westerners like Elaine Pagels and John Hick are on the same page.

The pluralists have read history and are troubled by the wars and persecutions done over the centuries in the name of religion. They long for the kind of understanding which will produce peace on earth.

Nevertheless, I was totally unprepared for what the monk had said. Almost every serious Buddhist I had ever talked to and most every book I had ever read on world religions had cautioned me to not try to package Buddhist beliefs in Christian concepts. Don't go looking for a god in Buddhism. There is none. Don't compare *Nibbana* (Nirvanna) with the Christian concept of heaven. It's totally different.

Trying to fit Christianity into Buddhist metaphysics or vice versa would be like Cinderella's sisters trying to squeeze their feet into glass slippers not made for them. Pluralists have good intentions, to be sure, but I always had trouble buying their argument. But here was a good hearted Buddhist monk who was challenging my view of reality.

The monk had piqued my interest. "How much is the book?"

I asked. "I'd really like to read it."

"You can have it," he replied.

"Wow. Thank you." This was genuine serendipity, maybe even more than a chance meeting. "By the way, who is Bikku Buddha Datu?"

I thought I saw the hint of a pleased smile as the monk pointed to himself.

2

CHARADES AND DISCO PEEING

As I was falling asleep in the bed the porter had made up for me on the overnight train to Chiang Mai, I was feeling a little proud of myself.

After a Cambodian pastor had brought me to the bus in Phnom Penh, I had already been on my own for two days. On the bus no one spoke English and I didn't know a word of Cambodian. Communicating was like playing charades with a lot of hand motions and facial expressions.

For example, when you get to be my age—63 at the time—you have to pee a lot more often than when you were in your twenties. About two hours into the six hour bus ride, I didn't feel like I could hold it any longer, so I got up out of my seat towards the front of the bus and started heading towards where I thought the toilet was located.

When the guy next to the driver--who amounted to a kind of co-pilot--saw me, a questioning look came on his face, so I motioned towards the back of the bus. He nodded to say he understood and then proceeded to help me navigate my way down the aisle while the bus was rocking and rolling down the road. The highways in Cambodia are not up to the standards of American interstates.

I carefully descended the narrow stairway leading to the lower level of the double decker bus and found myself in the midst of suitcases and shipping crates in the huge luggage compartment. I looked at the co-pilot—the guy was still with me--with a questioning look on my face, and he pointed to the other side of the luggage compartment. To get to where he was pointing, I had to get down on my hands and knees and crawl for eight feet to a little metal compartment which looked more like a small closet than a wash room.

What I found was a traditional southeast Asian toilet which is basically an enhanced hole in the floor which you straddle, squat over and do your business. . .while the bus is jerking rather violently from side to side. The Laotian pastor who was a co-leader on the trip I had just finished referred to this activity as *disco peeing*.

Relieved, in more ways than one, that the disco session had ended, I crawled back to the stairway and made my way back to the front of the bus. Wouldn't you know it? About twenty minutes later the bus pulled over to the side of the road, and most of the passengers got out, taking care of their business al fresco. Some walked into the rice field a short way but others just peed right there on the side of the road.

I felt a surge of pride. "Anyone can pee on terra firma," I thought, "but it takes a special talent to do it on a jerky roller coaster." As the trip continued I felt proud that I had made it to the border, had gotten through customs, had been able to communicate to the *tuk tuk* (a kind of three wheeled taxi) that I wanted lodging near the train station, had gotten dinner and had found a way to make it to the train on time the next morning—all on my own.

This is what I wanted. In the 40 days, more or less, between the end of the mission trip I had just finished and the beginning of the conference I would be attending south of Bangkok at the end of January, I wanted to experience the challenge of being largely on my own in a foreign culture. I wanted to bump up against something solid and see how I would respond, to be alone with my self and God and see what would happen.

As I fell asleep in the swaying train car—definitely more gentle than the disco session on the bus—I felt like, at least for the first two days of my adventure, both travelling companions had come through for me. I had successfully made it from Phnom Penh to Bangkok and was on my way to Chiang Mai. I had encountered a Buddhist monk in ways that tourists seldom experience. The encounter had been a bit disorienting, but that's exactly what I had been hoping for.

So as I fell asleep I felt a paradoxical satisfaction that I had met a challenge on my own and that, at the same time, God had been taking care of me.

3

Nicky and M

I got off the overnight train from Bangkok in Chiang Mai feeling confident. I set down my bags at the nearest bench, took out my mobile phone and punched in the number of one of the budget guest houses which my *Lonely Planet* guidebook had recommended.

"Hello. Is this Lamchang House? Do you have any rooms available? No? Um…OK. Thank you." Strange. I'd done this before in other towns with no problem. Always had vacancies. Shouldn't make any difference that this is the Christmas holiday season. Buddhists wouldn't be getting time off from their jobs to celebrate the birth of Jesus.

"Hello. Malak Guest House? Do you have any rooms available. No? OK. Thank you."

My self-assured, independent world traveler confidence began to wane as I heard the same response from the Jonadda Guest House, the Siri Guesthouse, the Thapae Gate Lodge and the Rendezvous Guest House.

I prayed, feeling a little silly to be thinking about talking to God only after I had started to feel desperate. "OK," I thought. "One more try."

Same answer from the Safe House Court. What do I do now? I knew the answer to that question, but my deflated ego urged me to keep trying to figure out some way to pull this thing off on my own.

Finally, I had to let go and admit that I needed help. I punched in the phone number of Phawinee Srilorm or Nicky as everyone called her. Thais seem to love western sounding nicknames.

"This is Tom, Nicky. I'm at the train station here in Chiang Mai, and I need your help." I had known Nicky for six years. Nicky had been my intern in Forest Park for three months in 2004, and she was a member of the Nong Bua Sam Church which over the years had become more or less my home congregation in Chiang Mai.

Nicky and M

After apologizing for bothering her on a Saturday, I explained the situation. She replied, "M (her fiancée) and I will be there in half an hour. We don't have anything we have to do today except take care of you."

I knew she would say that. After working with the Thai congregation back home for eighteen years and visiting Thailand seven times, I had grown accustomed to the welcome and generous hospitality I almost always received.

Nicky and M were right on time and greeted me with big smiles. I felt safe again and very much humbled.

"Have you eaten breakfast?"

"Not yet," I admitted.

"Good, we're hungry," Nicky said, "and we just found a good noodle place that's cheap."

Still wanting to prove that I was on top of my game, I said, "I'd like to pay."

"Oh, no, Pastor Holmes," M replied. "You are our guest. When we come to Chicago, you can pay."

I knew the chances of that ever happening were as great as the Cubs winning the World Series, but it would be very un-Thai to start an argument, so I just said, "Thank you."

We had a delicious meal of noodles after which Nicky and M informed me that I would be sleeping at the home of M and his mother, Kampan, until lodging could be found. After making a few phone calls, they informed me that Fon, another member of Nong Bua Sam, was working on finding a guest house for me.

Grace can be hard to accept. Sometimes gifts can be hard to receive. Thankfully, I received this gift without protest, but not without some significant internal struggle.

4

Joint Christmas Celebration

Nicky and M dropped me off at Kampan's house and told me that that evening they would be taking me to a Christmas fellowship event which would include five small Christian churches in their area. The five congregations do this every year a week before Christmas. I was tired and lay down for an hour nap. As I fell asleep I looked forward to the gathering and tried to imagine would it would be like.

I confess to having idealized fantasies of Christians in Thailand. Some of my prejudice for them is based on eighteen years of interacting with Thais. For the most part they have treated me as an honored guest. At the lunches Nong Bua Sam Church has after worship, they always have a special seat for me, and the women keep bringing me food—enough for two people. Usually they find a time in the service when Pastor Holmes can "greet" them, even when I'd been with them three Sundays in a row.

Part of it, however, is what I imagine must be true about a 1% minority in an overwhelmingly Buddhist land. In my mind they are like the early Christians—a persecuted minority whose suffering makes them strong in faith, steadfast in their love for each other and grateful for the spiritual security they have in the midst of the changes and chances of life.

That's how religious reformers throughout the history of the Christian church tend to describe what they are trying to do—to move church practice back to the way it was in the beginning.

A sweet dream. I was going to be with *real* Christians. Three days into what I had planned to be a solitary venture into a foreign culture where I thought I would be tested, I found myself being taken care of by old friends and getting ready to be with several hundred other Christians. So much for my plans, but maybe what I would be experiencing would be even better than what I had planned.

Years before, I had been complaining—again only half jokingly— to Andre Hines, our church council president, that God always answered my prayers but rarely the way I wanted. She looked at me straight in the eye, put her hands on her hips in mock disgust and replied, "That's because He's smarter than you are." I have tried not to forget Andre's wisdom.

The church hosting the event was a thirty minute drive from "M and Kampan's Guesthouse." The *soi* (lane) was blocked off to automobile traffic, and people were milling around with one hand holding bowls of fried rice and orange sodas in the other. M led me to a front row seat in the area where the program would take place in an hour later and brought me a plate full of food, after which he ran off to join Nicky who was leading a youth activity.

I didn't mind being left alone. The food was not so spicy that *farang* (foreigners) could not enjoy it. I had my camera, and as far as I could see there was only one non-Thai family in attendance besides me. This was the real thing, maybe better than what I was looking for, a good taste of what the early church had been like.

Disappointment began to set in when I noticed that the praise band was wearing red Santa Clause caps and playing Jingle Bells. It deepened when a church member came into view wearing a full Santa Clause outfit followed by a toddler dressed the same way.

I noticed that speakers were piled eight feet high on both sides of the stage, and when the program began, they cranked them up to at least half capacity which was 25% more than was comfortable for me.

21

I became encouraged when the program began with eight beautiful young women dressed in traditional silk costumes performed a classical dance to welcome the Christ child. Then, the host church proceeded to put on a Christmas pageant more impressive than anything we'd been able to pull off back home. I would have preferred that the program be less technological and more purely Thai until it dawned on me that in 2010 this was authentically Thai. Maybe the program would turn out to be OK after all.

My lingering disappointment, however, turned to disillusionment when at the end of the pageant, a drum roll came over the tower of speakers, and two men dressed as reindeer pulled through the compound entrance a two wheeled cart in which a Santa, complete with a faux white beard, was seated.

The crowd went nuts. Children rushed the stage, and the jolly old elf pulled bags of candy out of his sack which he distributed to the kids.

Now, I have nothing against Santa, but I know for a fact that he was not part of the Christmas celebrations of the early church. The early church, I had learned, probably had not made a big deal of Christmas to begin with. The host church was not cooperating with my fantasies. They were trying to be relevant, to connect with twenty-first century Thai people, and I wanted what I imagined to be real almost two thousand years ago.

That I had not notified them in advance of how I wanted them to design the evening's program didn't dawn on me at the time. What I knew was that MY NEEDS, or what I thought were my needs, were not being met.

When Nicky and M said it was time to return to M's Guesthouse, I was happy to leave the party.

5

KAMPAN'S PORCH

Kampan's house is on a *soi* (lane) in what I'll call a sub rural area thirty minutes from the Old City in central Chiang Mai. The *soi* is flanked by middle class homes interspersed with groves of *langkom* and rice paddies. Ten minutes can go by without a car or motorbike passing.

Nicky, M and I ate a breakfast of rice soup and fresh fruit seated on a reed mat on the floor of their outdoor kitchen. It was Monday morning, so both got ready to leave for work after cleaning up the breakfast dishes.

I asked M to drop me off at the local Buddhist *wat* (temple complex) on his way to work. I wanted to snoop around the *wat* and then stroll back to my temporary guesthouse, taking pictures along the way.

Kampan's outdoor kitchen

The local Wat

I explored the *wat* for half an hour, and as I was leaving, I was greeted by a Nong Bua Sam member who lived right across the *soi* from the temple. I figured out that M and told her to look after this *farang* who might get lost. She did her duty in greeting me, but what she really wanted to do was show off her home. I took a picture of her standing in front of the house and said it was *sawai* (beautiful) in my best Thai which I think she understood. At any rate, we smiled a lot which communicated more than my bad Thai.

I took pictures of coconut palms, front yards full of flowers and the one or two picturesque homes on the lane made of wood instead of cement. About half a mile down the *soi*, another church member came out of her home with a glass of water on a silver tray. M had been busy. We smiled a lot—Thailand is billed as the *Land of Smiles* by the chamber of commerce—and I thanked her for her concern.

A glass of water?   *Soi outside Kampan's house5*

Ten minutes later a man on a bicycle stopped and, I think, asked me if I was OK. This guy was not recruited by M. He apparently had not heard via the village grapevine that this old *farang* was staying at M and Kampan's place. I think he eventually understood me when I explained where I was going. Smiles again.

By this time of the morning the sun was hot, so after downing half a bottle of water, I quickly found a comfortable place to sit on the front porch where I could do my morning prayers and read. Kampan's front yard was really a garden filled with flowers and ferns and shaded by a huge tree.

Kampan's porch

At first I felt some restlessness. In my adult life I'd been able to travel to Rome, Austria, Germany, Puerto Rico, Mexico, Hawaii and Alaska. In every case I would get up and be out the door early in a frantic attempt to see "everything"—motivated by a kind of neurotic fear that if I missed one of the attractions listed in the guide book as "must see" I'd never be able to forgive myself.

Kampan's porch and front yard are not listed in any of the guide books. Was I missing something by being stuck out in the country for a few days?

I looked up frequently from my reading, sometimes to watch a man on a motorbike passing by, at other times to simply enjoy the flowers. I felt my muscles relaxing. My mind shifted into neutral, a state in which I wasn't thinking about anything. I watched a gecko on the wall. I gazed at the flowers in the yard. I watched a neighbor ride his motorbike into his driveway. When he noticed me he made a *wai* (Thai greeting gesture with palms together) to me and I *waied* him back.

The neighbor went into his house, but his cat decided to come over and check me out. He took his time, making it clear that he could take me or leave me. When he got about fifteen feet from me, he stopped and with his tail twitching started to look me over. . .until a movement in the canopy of the big tree distracted him.

26

Spotting a squirrel, the cat transformed from the neighbor's pet into a ferocious predator. He was channeling, I think, the tiger he had been in a previous lifetime. This was, after all, a Buddhist cat.

The squirrel in the branches above being more interesting than the *farang* on the porch, the cat began to climb the tree. Although I'm sure the squirrel was aware of the cat's approach, he continued playing in the branches. By now the cat was really into the hunt, slowly, carefully creeping towards what promised to be a delicious dinner.

When the cat got within ten feet of his fantasy meal, the squirrel decided to end the game and scampered down a thin branch, leaped to the roof of Kampan's house and disappeared from view.

By this time, the cat was two-thirds of the way up the tree, and it suddenly dawned on him that while his claws were formed in a way that made climbing up the tree relatively easy, getting down without slipping was an entirely different matter. The cat froze. It was one of those "oh crap, what do I do now" moments.

The first challenge for the former tiger was simply turning around on the slender limb he had gone out on. It reminded me of the situation many politicians have found themselves in recently. After tentatively trying different contortions, he finally got his body going in the right direction, and for a good five minutes I watched one vulnerable, scared feline extricate himself from the predicament he'd gotten himself into.

By that time I had lost track of time. For I'm not sure how many hours I had not thought many thoughts, and that felt good. I had just taken in what had been going on around me. I felt embarrassed when I realized that in my younger days I would have called this a wasted day.

I recalled that during my prayer time that morning I read the beginning of the fortieth chapter of Isaiah, the last verse of which declared, "They who wait on the Lord shall renew their strength." It was still the season of Advent which in liturgical churches is a time to focus on, among other things, waiting for the surprises God has in store for his people.

What I had experienced that day on the *soi* and on Kampan's porch made me think of a passage from one of my devotional books:

"Why are you rushing so much?" asked the rabbi.
"I'm rushing after my livelihood," the man answered.
"And how do you know," said the rabbi, "that your livelihood is running on before you, so that you have to rush after it? Perhaps it's behind you, and all you need to do is stand still."
Tale about Rabbi Ben Meir of Berdichev

Molly Wolf put it this way in *From White China: Finding the Divine in the Everyday* (in Spring, p. 12):
It [mud season or spring] is a witness to slowness, groundedness, and living with the moment, however unlovely the moment may seem. It begs for patience, a virtue most of us need to cultivate anyway, and for a richer understanding of how this earth really works. So I've learned to treasure mud season—at least occasionally. When I get fed up with it, I find there's usually some God-Stuff lurking under last fall's leaves, if I'm willing to look.

6

BUDDHIST CUB SCOUTS

Thirty Cub Scouts—all in uniform—respectfully entered the Nong Bua Sam Church on a Tuesday afternoon, four days before Dec. 25. They were on their winter vacation, so their four leaders decided to take these Buddhist first and second graders on a field trip to the local Christian church to learn more about Christmas.

Cub Scouts at Nong Bua Sam Church

The church was already decorated with a life size manger scene and poinsettias. When the boys and girls were all seated on the floor, Nicky and M led half an hour of clap along songs which were blatantly Christian. The Cub Scouts got into the songs immediately, doing all the motions they were taught.

After the singing, these Buddhist youngsters watched a twenty minute animated telling of the Christmas story. Other than a few of the kids squirming, because the video got too long, they watched with interest.

Once again, I hadn't expected what I was seeing. I had been clinging to a picture of this tiny Christian minority courageously living out their faith in an overwhelmingly Buddhist land. What I saw was thirty youngsters enjoying a couple hours in a church, and their leaders approving of the whole program. The leaders had been there several times before, so it wasn't like they didn't know what they were getting into.

Nicky and M ended the program by playing a couple silly games with the children and then leading them outdoors where they were treated to ice cream.

When I talked to Sanit Katika, or Elder Sanit as the Nong Bua Sam members call him, about what had happened that evening, he told me that Buddhists and Christians get along fine in Thailand. Christians are accepted and even respected as good neighbors.

Perhaps the good feeling continues because Thai Buddhists don't feel threatened by Christians. Catholic missionaries have been in Thailand since the 1500s and Protestants have been working there since in 1828, but the Christian population in Thailand remains at 1%.

H.R.H. Prince Damrong, in an introductory chapter he wrote in English for a volume published in 1928 celebrating 100 years of Protestant missionary work in Thailand, said, "I appreciate the request [to write a chapter] as one arising from friendship based on mutual respect and confidence."

Damrong noted that the missionaries no longer "abuse Buddhism" as a tactic in their attempt to convert Thais to Christianity and commended the missionaries of his day for "their sterling qualities and the good work they have done in educational and medical matters. . . ." (McFarland, p. 15)

If success is determined by numbers, the Christian venture in

Thailand has been a miserable failure. I began to wonder what keeps Sanit and the Nong Bua Sam Christians going when their efforts "to make disciples of all nations" achieve such minimal results. . . .until I realized that my definition of success is very Western indeed.

I haven't kept coming back to this small church on a quiet *soi* in sub rural Thailand since 1994 because they are successful in terms of numbers. I have returned year after year because there, half way around the world, I've felt loved.

I think I began to understand why Sanit, Nicky, M and the other Nong Bua Sam members don't lose heart. Their goal is not "to win people for Christ" as some Christians I know would articulate it, and therefore they don't keep score.

Their goal is to introduce people they meet to someone they love and who loves them, realizing that it is not up to them to try to convert or manipulate people into loving him the same way they do.

7

WRESTLING WITH BHIKKU BUDDHA DHATU

Fon had found a guesthouse for me, the Riverside B and B right on the Ping River in central Chiang Mai. Kampan and M's "guesthouse" had been a gift, but now I was really alone again—where I had wanted to be.

Courtyard at the Riverside Guest House

One of the advantages of being alone was that I had more time to read, so I took out the book that Bhikkhu Buddha Dhatu, the monk I talked to in Bangkok, gave me and was at last able to try to figure out how he could say that all religions are the same.

As I got into *The Truth of the Messengers*, I think I understood what the old monk was saying—basically that all religions are the same in terms of the ethics they teach. He wrote,

> All religions are the same—all teach the same precepts and all religious teachers say the same things: avoid evil, do good, keep your thoughts pure, do unto others what you would want others to do to you, you reap what you sow etc. etc. (p. 121)

Indeed, the *Five Precepts* that Buddhism teaches the lay people to keep—

1. Do not kill
2. Do not steal
3. Do not engage in sexual misconduct
4. Do not lie
5. Do not drink alcohol

—sound very much the Bible's Ten Commandments except for precept number five, and indeed some Christian churches think that should be number eleven.

I found some things in *The Truth of the Messengers* that did sound very much like what I had heard in some churches.

- ❖ People today are blinded by money and their desires for a luxurious life and do not realize that at death, they lose everything...
- ❖ If our minds are free of hate, anger and delusion, we would be better off than kings and presidents. Many rich people are poor in their minds; many poor people are rich in theirs.
- ❖ People say that our society is modern and progressive....Yet, the world is full of materialism and selfishness and people do nothing much more than strive to survive the rat race.

As I read further, I discovered that Dhatu pictured himself as a reformer. He was especially critical of how many monks were behaving, much like Jesus had condemned the Pharisees. He even contended that some of the worst of them would be reincarnated as dogs. "No, not just dogs," he ranted. "Even insects."

I had retained enough anti-authoritarianism from the sixties to resonate with that attitude a little bit, although he also elicited some of my fear of judgment, because I know I hadn't always lived up to Jesus' standards.

I also learned that many Thai Buddhists think of their religion as having two tracks. If you were a lay person, the most you could hope for was to be reborn into a better position next time around. Forget about *Nibbana* (Nirvana).

A lay person is too distracted by the responsibilities and stresses of life to be "free of desires, attachments, anger and delusions." "As laypeople," Dhatu reasoned, "your days and nights are filled with the problems of survival in this materialistic, dog eat dog society. How then can you meditate well?"

In contrast, he argued, the role of the *Sangha* (the community of monks) is to detach from all the cares of making this impermanent life work. "The sole duty of the *Sangha*," he declared, "is to strive for enlightenment, for *Nibbana*, and then, to show others how to do the same."

Having been brought up in a religious tradition that taught that pastors were just as human and sinful as lay people, I had a hard time buying that one. What was even harder for me to understand was *kamma* (karma).

Dhatu defined *kamma* as "action leading to future reward or retribution." It's "you reap what you sow" to the max. In Buddhism, there is no room for randomness or luck. If you are receiving good, you must have done good...in a previous life or in this one. If you are suffering, well, that's what you get for not following the precepts.

Dhatu, and every other Buddhist teacher I've ever heard or read, insists that what you become in the future is all up to you. Buddhism is often called a non-theistic religion. It really is all up to you.

The reason *kamma* is hard for me to swallow is that in 1998 I was diagnosed with a progressive neurological disorder called Primary Lateral Sclerosis which left me disabled and unable to continue functioning in what I considered to be my vocation. This, even though my whole life I had exercised, eaten right, gotten enough sleep and done nothing to shame my parents! In other words, I had been a good boy—not without sin by any means, but having done nothing to deserve this.

So when Harold Kushner's book, *When Bad Things Happen to Good People*, came out I was one of the first to buy it. On top of that, I had been raised in the Lutheran tradition which taught that we sinners are saved by God's unmerited grace. If a book had been published entitled *Why Good Things Happen to Bad People*, it would have been written by a Lutheran.

In other words, I had no problem seeing randomness and surprise, bad luck and grace in life. And, the notion of having done something in a previous life, even if were true, didn't help me deal with my PLS in this life.

And that's the way it has often gone when I've crossed cultural boundaries. I got one of my questions raised by Bhikku Buddha Dhatu—his statement about all religions being the same--answered by reading his book, only to have several others raised.

8

Good Day Alone, Bad Day Alone

I woke up the next morning refreshed. Temperatures at night in Chiang Mai in "winter" dip into the sixties. The breakfast at the Riverside B and B consisted of coffee, toast and fresh fruit: mango, pineapple and two of those short, fat bananas which taste so good.

I had the day all planned out. I was going to pick up where I left off on my train ride from Bangkok. I would get back to testing myself by trying to function alone in this foreign country.

After breakfast I would begin by hailing a *tuk tuk*, those three wheeled open air taxis in which the driver sits in front with the stick shift between his legs and the two passengers—three if they are slender Thais—sit on a bench in the back. They make a sound like a loud baritone mosquito which burps, coughs and sputters when the driver lets up on the throttle.

Tuk Tuk in Chiang Mai

As far as exhaust fumes go, let's just say *tuk tuks* would not pass EPA standards back in the USA. They are loud and not very comfortable. Riders breathe in fumes for the whole trip, but they're great fun and a cheap way to get around.

I had my little speech memorized. *"Pom bpai Wat Phra Sihng."* Hooray! The *tuk tuk* driver understood me, so I tried some more Thai. *"Thao rai?* (how much)?" I asked.

"Hok sip baht (Sixty baht)," he replied.

"OK," I said, and we were off to the temple complex I had been to one other time on a previous trip. I remembered it being less overrun by tourists, which is what I wanted. I love hanging out at the temple complexes known as *wats*. They provide a feast of color for the amateur photographer in me, and they always have gardens or at least shady areas where it is pleasant to read, pray or just hang out.

"Wat Phra Sihng," announced my driver as we entered the temple complex. Anxious that he be patient with me as I struggled to find a way to get out of the back seat, I said, *"Cha chaa* (slowly)."

"Cha chaa," he repeated with a smile. He understood me again! Yes!

After hanging out at the temple for an hour or so, I found another *tuk tuk* waiting for a rider under a tree by the temple gate. *"Pom bpai Suriwong Book Center,"* I said, this time with a little confidence. *"Tao rai?"*

"Hok sip baht," he replied.

"Am I bi-lingual or what?" I thought as I slowly climbed into the back seat saying, *"Cha chaa."*

"Cha chaa." He smiled.

Wat Phra Sihng

I like shopping at Suriwong, because it has the largest section of books in Chiang Mai in English about Thailand or by Thai authors. I loaded my back pack with eight new titles.

Back outside, I caught another *tuk tuk*, this time to the Anusan Market which is part of Chiang Mai's huge night bazaar. There I enjoyed an order of mango and sticky rice at my favorite open air restaurant and followed that up with a banana *rotee* from the Muslim lady who fries them up at a stand right next to the restaurant.

A final five minute *tuk tuk* ride and I was back at the Riverside guesthouse. I had made it through the whole day using, for the most part, only Thai. I felt in control. I felt on top of my game. I felt like I had prepared myself well for this adventure, practiced my Thai, was realistic in my expectations and now was experiencing the "thrill of victory". . .or something a little more modest than that.

The degree to which I feel in control determines, to a great extent, my internal emotional weather. When I feel in control, my spirits rise. Out of control and powerless, I get depressed. As I crawled under the blanket in my bed with the window above me open to let in the cool night air, I felt the same way I had felt on the overnight train from Bangkok. I had faced a challenge by myself and passed the test.

*　　　*　　　*

Two days later I tried more or less the same program, except this time the *tuk tuk* driver had a hard time understanding where I wanted to go. "*Wat Suan Dok*," I kept repeating.

Finally after about six tries on my part, his face brightened in recognition. "*Wat Suan Dok!*" he exclaimed, nodding his head.

"That's what I said," I thought to myself, knowing full well that I had mispronounced the name of the temple. It's hard enough for *farang* (westerners) to get the pronunciations right when trying to speak Thai, because it's a tonal language. The word *mai*, for example, can mean *new, mile, right?, silk* or *no* depending on if the tone is low, mid, high, rising or falling.

What makes pronouncing Thai words doubly difficult for me is my slurred speech caused by my PLS. Some folks even have a hard time understanding me when I'm trying to speak English!

When I got to *Wat Suan Dok*, I was disappointed. I couldn't see why *Lonely Planet* had recommended it. No photogenic scenes. No garden or even a shade tree to loaf under. I was hungry. The *tuk tuk* trip getting there had been long. I had gotten a late start, and in an hour the sun would set.

I did my penguin waddle with my cane out to the road outside the gate and waited for a *tuk tuk*. Five minutes. Ten minutes. Fifteen minutes. This was a main road, Thanon Suthep, but no *tuk tuk*.

Finally a *sawng taeou* (a pick up truck with two benches in the rear and a roof) came by, and I waved for it to stop. "*Thanon Nawarat*," I said to the driver, and after the fourth try he nodded. I crawled into the back of the truck and smiled at the other two passengers already on board. I didn't feel like smiling just then, but it is the Thai thing to do.

Sawng Tae Ou

The *sawng taeou* drove around Chiang Mai for half an hour, dropping the two passengers off and picking others up along the way. Sometimes I recognized landmarks. At other times I didn't. Minute by minute I was losing trust that the driver really understood where I wanted to go. Finally, in a panic, I decided to cut my losses and get out before traveling even further away from the Riverside B and B. I pulled the rope which signals the driver that a passenger wants to get out.

After crawling out *cha chaa* and paying the driver, I looked around and realized that I had chosen to get out at a spot where there was little traffic. I stood at a corner, praying for a *sawng taeou* or *tuk tuk* to pass by whose driver could understand my Thai.

After twenty minutes of solitary waiting, I began thinking of worst case scenarios. "I suppose I could curl up on the sidewalk for the night," I thought. "I have my jacket along in my back pack."

At that point a lady crossed the street and approached me. In Thai she asked me how she could help, and, in response, I repeated the same memorized speech I had given the *sawng taeou* driver almost an hour before. No matter how slowly I spoke, she could not understand what I was saying. Then another woman crossed the street and tried to help. In a short time I was surrounded by six earnest Thais, all doing their best to help this stranded *farang* get to where he wanted to go.

When a *sawng taeou* finally appeared, all six jumped in the road in front of the truck to make it stop. I repeated "*Thanon Nawarat*" to the driver with the same result.

Then the thought crossed my mind: "What would the Buddha tell me do?"

"Calm down and detach," was the answer I came up with. Well, calming down couldn't hurt anything, so I gave it a try. All the while, seven Thais and I were playing charades and talking slowly trying to solve my problem

Then I had another thought. "What would Jesus do?" He certainly wouldn't be against calming down, I thought, and would probably tell me to trust him.

It was then that I had an inspiration. Instead of trying to tell the driver that I wanted to go to *Thanon Nawarat*—a strategy that was clearly not working—why don't I say a location that was very well known and was at least a lot closer to the Riverside B and B than I was now, so I said, "Night Bazaar. *Pom bpai Night Bazaar.*"

An international break through immediately occurred. "Night Bazaar," everyone said in chorus in a mutual flash of understanding. The driver smiled and nodded. I crawled in the back, and within five minutes was at a place in the night market where I knew the *tuk tuk* drivers were familiar with the location of the Riverside guesthouse.

As I crawled under the covers, a wave of relief swept over me. I was home. Well, not exactly home, but at least a place where I felt I had regained a little control. I wasn't feeling down, exactly, but certainly didn't feel the buzz I felt the night before. More like humbled and sobered. A pattern seemed to be getting established.

9

Christmas in Chiang Mai

Part of the baggage I brought with me to Thailand at the beginning of December was this fantasy that alone in Thailand, away from the commercialism of the holidays in America, I would somehow find the true meaning of Christmas.

I woke up at the guest house along the Ping River in Chiang Mai on Christmas Eve to discover that the temperature had plummeted to a "chilly" 65 degrees during the night. All the Thais were whining about how cold it was. I just shook my head.

I had more important things to do. This was the day I had been looking forward to. This was the day on which I was to gain enlightenment, as it were, the day I would discover the true meaning of Christmas.

I walked through the guest house garden to the open air dining area to be greeted by a recording of Elvis Presley singing *Blue, Blue Christmas* followed by *Silent Night, Jingle Bells, The First Noel, I'm Dreaming of a White Christmas, and Joy to the World*. It was an inn which catered to Americans and Europeans, so it was understandable that an establishment run by Buddhists would be playing Christmas music.

But then I remembered my visit to the Airport Plaza the day before, a mall similar to Water Tower Place on Michigan Avenue, where a giant Christmas tree towered up to the ceiling in the mall's five story atrium, and Christmas music played on the shopping center's loud speakers.

The Thais have discovered that Christmas can be good for business. Trees with lights, inflated plastic snowmen, gift wrapping and images of riding in a one horse open sleigh are good for business—never mind that many Thais have never seen snow let alone know what a one horse open sleigh is. It felt kind of unreal in way—Thais loving songs about a winter wonderland and the birth of the Son of God.

Christmas tree at Airport Plaza

Peter, Paul and Mary had a hit song forty years ago called *I Dig Rock and Roll Music*. One line in the song goes "and the words don't get in the way." That's the way it seems to be for Thais. Christmas for them is kind of a Disney World fantasy land to which you can escape the day to day struggles of life and have fun for awhile.

Thais love having fun. They call it *sanuk*. *Sanuk* means spicing up everything you do with teasing and jokes and light heartedness. It's kind of like their cuisine which is based on noodles and rice—very bland ingredients. Until, that is, you add the chili peppers and spices for which the Thais are famous and then the flavor in your mouth shouts, "Wow."

After breakfast I sat in the guesthouse garden, and tried to get into my spiritual task by reading the Christmas stories in Luke and Matthew. As I read about Joseph and Mary, who was nine months pregnant, trudging for several days from Nazareth to Bethlehem;

Mary giving birth in a smelly barn; and the family running for their lives to Egypt because an insecure king named Herod was out to kill their baby; it dawned on me that there is very little *sanuk* in the story which started this whole Christmas thing in the first place.

It's like we can't handle reality, like we're always looking for an escape. It's true for religious people who have romanticized the Christmas story into a cute cartoon. It's true for secular folk who focus on giving presents and having fun during the holidays, who somehow in the midst of the freezing temperatures and slippery ice of December can conjure up a romantic vision of a winter wonderland.

The original Christmas story—you know, the one without Santa, Rudolf and Christmas cards—is not an escape from reality but an attempt to embrace it in a transforming way. No escape in the original.

As the day wore on I began to miss home more and more. I confess that I did miss my two children and opening presents on Christmas Eve. I missed the prospect of Christmas dinner with turkey and dressing and homemade Christmas cookies.

But what I missed most of all was community—that group of people I saw Sunday after Sunday who were in church trying to discover meaning for their lives in the Bible stories, who were struggling to find strength to live out what they believed in the midst of an ambiguous reality which is anything but a winter wonderland.

I missed singing Christmas carols with people for whom the words to *Silent Night* and *Joy to the World* didn't get in the way but meant a great deal.

10

CHRISTMAS DAY

Christmas Eve hadn't gone according to my plans. Instead of achieving enlightenment regarding the true meaning of Christmas, I wound up missing my children, friends and church.

I thought I would be able to escape the commercialism back home by coming to a Buddhist country and instead was greeted by Christmas trees and *Merry Christmas* signs in many of the businesses, including my guest house. I wouldn't have been surprised to see a *Happy Holidays* banner in a Buddhist temple. Thankfully, I did not.

OK, so today I could try again. I would be alone until 3:00 in the afternoon when Nicky would pick me up to take me out to Kampan's house for the night. According to my fantasy, being alone would be the key to making my contact with God stronger. No distractions.

I decided to spend the morning reading the Christmas story in Luke and Matthew again. Then, I'd go to the first chapter of John to read his more theological and less narrative account and finish off with Philippians 2, the part about Christ not hanging on to equality with the Father but humbling himself and taking on human form.

During breakfast at the guest house I heard from Elvis and Bing and Alvin and the Chipmunks again. I couldn't wait to get away from that "feel good" music, and be by myself. After I finished my toast and fresh papaya, I walked over to a nearby coffee shop, sat on the porch, took out my Bible and tried to get into the spirit of Christmas.

Maybe it was because I was distracted by Alvin singing "I still want a hula hoop" over and over in my head, or maybe I was suffering from a kind of "depression hang-over" brought on by my disappointments from the day before, but I couldn't get into the Bible readings. . .even though I was alone. I'd start reading "in those days a decree went out. . ." and before I'd get through five verses, my mind would wander. So, I'd reprimand myself and start back at the beginning, get distracted and start back at the beginning, get distracted. . . .

A Buddhist I had read compared those random thoughts which intrude on your meditating to snakes which invade your house. "You have to drive the snakes out," he had written. So, I tried driving the random thoughts out of my mind, resulting in me getting more fixated on them than before.

The more I tried to make the Bible stories make me aware of God's presence, the further away from God I felt. Most Protestant Christians believe that God can reveal himself through any means he chooses—nature or other people or a novel—but that the least ambiguous communication is through the Bible. However, on this particular Christmas morning in the Year of our Lord 2010, or 2554 according to the Buddhist calendar, the Bible didn't seem to be opening any doors for me. I wasn't feeling anything "spiritual."

After an hour I threw in the towel and conceded that the snakes had won this round. I flagged down a *tuk tuk* and got dropped off at the huge wholesale flower market across the Ping River and just a kilometer north of the Riverside B&B. Better to do something positive than to spin my spiritual wheels.

The flower market turned out to be a pleasant break from my struggle to connect with God. Everywhere I pointed my camera there was a good picture. Vibrant color for more than one city block. And no Merry Christmas banners anywhere. "This is the real Thailand," I thought, "unspoiled by Western consumerism." Sure, they were buying and selling, but there was an easy going non-competitive feel to the activity going on in the open air stalls, almost as if the interaction was more important to them than the bottom line.

Flower market at Chiang Mai

By the time Nicky picked me up, I no longer felt depressed or disappointed. I had to admit, though, that I was glad to have company on Christmas Day. On the way out to Kampan's house, Nicky told me that Elder Sanit and Jiraporn had invited everyone from the Nong Bua Sam Church to their home for fellowship that evening. Being alone hadn't gotten me into the Christmas spirit. Maybe being with other believers would.

Nong Bua Sam is only a hundred meters down the *soi* from Kampan's house, and since many of the members were at the church getting ready for their Christmas celebration which they would hold the next day, I asked Nicky to drop me off at the church.

Since there was nothing I could do to help, I hung out with the members who were preparing 500 bags of goodies for the neighborhood kids. Most of the children around the church are Buddhist, but they know where the candy is at Christmas time.

Even though I understood very little of what was being said, the energy and excitement which accompanied the making of preparations felt very familiar. It was how I had spent the last thirty years of my life—planning children's pageants, writing sermons, getting ready for the big day. The feeling wasn't exactly spiritual, but it was good.

As I looked around I noticed how many beautiful faces were surrounding me. It was very much like my experience at the flower market a few hours earlier. There was beauty everywhere. So, of course, I took out my camera and started taking pictures.

There happened to be six girls helping assemble the gift bags who seemed to be around fourteen years old and who were especially attractive to me. I could just imagine their faces in the slide show I would be putting together after returning to Chicago. But when I pointed my camera at one of them, she lowered her head, so I couldn't see her face. Thinking she was just shy, I pointed the camera at the girl next to her who turned her head away.

Strange. I was used to Thais being very responsive to cameras, making the peace sign and flashing big smiles, and then giggling when I showed them the image on the camera's screen. These girls, however, wouldn't join in the *sanuk*, the fun. In fact, they seemed irritated with me, like I was violating their personal space.

After a couple minutes of trying to coax at least one of them to pose for me, I got the not so subtle hint and put my camera away. It happens often when I'm in Thailand. My instincts are not very good in that culture so different from mine.

At 8:00 that evening twenty of the older members of Nong Bua Sam and I assembled at the home of Sanit and Jiraporn. Everyone took off their shoes at the door and took their place in a circle of chairs and couches in the living room. Many were dressed in red, some even wearing stocking caps embroidered with reindeer.

Christmas at Sanit and Jiraporn's house

We sang Christmas carols—they in Thai and I in English—prayed together (in Thai, none of which I understood) and received tins of cookies from our hosts on the way out. In Thai culture, gifts are often given. Singing the carols, receiving a gift, being with people who shared my sense of what this day means, it all felt a little bit better than my battles with the snakes earlier that day. But only a little better and a long, long way from enlightenment.

Back at Kampan's house, I gave my host a *wai*, said good night and went straight to bed.

11

Birds of a Feather. . . .

I walked the hundred meters from Kampan's house to the Nong Bua Sam Church right after breakfast. I wanted to get there early to make sure I had time to get focused, or centered as the people who do meditation like to say.

Nong Bua Sam Church in Hang Dong (outside Chicang Mai)

Elder Sanit was playing Christmas music through the church's big speakers which he had placed outside the church. He was going to make sure that his Buddhist neighbors knew that this was the day on which the church was going to celebrate the birth of Jesus, especially if their children hadn't already reminded them that there were bags of candy waiting for them there.

The service began with a Christmas pageant, starring Nicky as Mary and M as Joseph. The fact that I had known both of them for years and that the little play itself felt so familiar raised my hopes that at last I might be able to get into the spirit of Christmas. Even though the congregation sang the carols in Thai, I knew enough of the words by heart—at least the first verses anyway—that I could sing along. . .the first verse over and over and over.

Christmas altar at Nong Bua Sam

At the beginning of the service, the church was full, but at the end of the pageant the announcement was made that ice cream would be served to the children and the bags of treats would be distributed outside. Half the congregation disappeared along with much of the energy in the room. Then, I realized that no one was present who could translate the sermon for me, and, in my experience, Thai sermons can last forty minutes.

So there I sat with no idea of what was being said, feeling bored and disappointed. I've been to exciting baseball games at Wrigley Field where I didn't notice how hard the wooden benches in the bleachers were, because I was so into the game. Exciting is not the word I would use to describe the service.

"No one is thinking about how I feel," I whined to myself. My butt was sore. I wanted to ask, "Are we there yet?" And, of course, by this time my bladder was full.

When the service ended, I headed straight for the bathroom

where I felt instant relief. Relieved was also how I felt about the service—relieved that it was over. These people who had welcomed me for so many years, who treated me like a king every time I was with them, couldn't stir up in me the feeling that I wanted. I felt at home with them in an important way, but no matter how hard they tried, they couldn't speak "my language."

So, when a missionary I knew, who was driving me home, invited me to join him and his family later that day at a service in English at a church just a kilometer down the road from my guesthouse, I jumped at the chance.

The *farang* (Westerners) congregation rented the space from a Thai church. Ninety-five percent of those in attendance where white. I understood every word. The sermon was blessedly short. The songs were familiar. I felt like I knew what the socially acceptable things to say and do were. I was a fish who was back in its cultural water.

I got back to my room around 7:00 pm, stretched out on the bed and got back into *Bangkok Eight*, a murder mystery set in Thailand. In the novel, a Thai detective named Sonchai, who is a devout Buddhist, keeps interacting with a blond, blue eyed American FBI agent named Kimberly Jones.

The sexual attraction between them is evident from the first time they meet, but they never get anywhere close to being intimate, because they keep missing each other culturally. She approaches problems rationally. He takes a more intuitive approach. Kimberly is secular. Sonchai is deeply religious. She is a feminist, while he thinks in more traditional terms.

"At least Sonchai can speak English," I thought as I let myself flow with the narrative. "At least they could communicate about the cultural differences that divided them."

And then I had a realization. It wasn't the enlightenment I was looking for about the true meaning of Christmas, but it was the one I was given that evening. No wonder Thais in Chicago will drive for up to an hour to attend the services of the Thai congregation which worshiped in our building.

It was a place where once a week they could relate to God and to each other in their "heart language." It wasn't just that they could speak in Thai, but it was also a place where all the cultural cues were familiar, where after church they could taste curries and nuclear strength peppers again and get the jokes that were being told.

Being an alien in a foreign land is hard work.

12

REALLY ON MY OWN

I woke up the next morning with a feeling that now the time alone I was anticipating was beginning for real. I had been alone off and on during the past eight days, but I always had something planned with Nicky, M or Sanit waiting for me within a day or two.

Now, except for Sunday mornings at Nong Bua Sam, I would really be on my own. Partly because my disability slows me down and partly because I wanted to digest everything I experienced, I plotted out a leisurely daily routine.

❖ Get up around 7:30
❖ Feast on fresh fruit at the breakfast provided by the guesthouse
❖ Check my email
❖ Around 10:00 catch a *tuk tuk* and explore Chiang Mai
❖ Relax in the shade of the big tree in the guesthouse courtyard
❖ Walk to a nearby mom and pop restaurant for a real Thai dinner
❖ Read in my room till bed time

The place I chose to explore was *Wat Chiang Man*, reputed to be the oldest *wat* (temple complex) in town. I never cease to marvel at how much I love just being in *wats*, even though the religion practiced there is alien to me. The architecture is stunning—*wihans* (large buildings with a Buddha statue for meditating) decorated in vibrant shades of red, gold, orange and white; gold leafed *chedis* pointing towards the sky; *kutis* (monk's quarters); and usually flowers and shade trees under which people can simply hang out.

Wat Chiang Man

One friend back home, when looking at my Thailand slides, remarked, "The Christian churches in Thailand look rather plain and uninteresting compared to the Buddhist temples." She's right. I never see tourists taking pictures of Christian churches in Thailand.

I have thought about the architectural differences a lot and have come to the conclusion that Christian church buildings in Thailand are designed to be functional, i.e. they are built not to look at but to DO something in them. It's when a community of people fills them that they become attractive. Buddhist *wats* are designed more as places to BE in. Churches are constructed with pews and pianos so that congregations can worship together. *Wats* are designed for individuals to come to as individuals and just be there alone in an environment conducive to meditating.

"These Buddhists are on to something we Christians don't understand very well," I thought. Silence; quieting the mind; solitude without loneliness; meditative environments. I realized that it is not realistic to go to a lot of effort creating an outside environment where I live when to sit in one between November and March would lead to hypothermia. But still. . . .

I took pictures at *Wat Chiang Man*, sat under a shade tree and more or less let my mind go blank as I took in everything around me. It felt similar to when I was hanging out on Kampan's porch. I took more pictures, snacked on some of the cookies I had received from Sanit and Jiraporn, read my Bible, prayed and took more pictures.

Around 4:00 I flagged down a *tuk tuk*, got off at my guesthouse and walked a block down Thanon Chiang Mai Lamphun to a parking lot where a mom and pop open air restaurant with seven small tables was tucked into a corner. I ordered green curry and rice, which the menu said would cost 30 baht (about a dollar) and a Pepsi.

When the Pepsi arrived, I realized that it was warm. That's why the glass the server gave me had ice in it. In the US that's not an issue, of course, but in Thailand it is the occasion for a big decision. You see, Montezuma lives in Thailand as well as in Mexico, and he loves to take revenge on those who drink the water.

So, the question becomes, "Has this ice been made from water that has been purified or has it come straight from the tap?" I knew how to say *ice* in Thai, but hadn't yet learned how to say *purified water*. There I sat, staring at a big bowl of green curry and chicken, trying to make a decision regarding whether to drink the Pepsi warm or go native and risk sitting on the toilet all night.

"What would the Buddha say?" I thought. I couldn't recall an answer in the *Dhamma* (Buddha's teaching) about this particular question. "What would Jesus do?" Same conclusion. I was left, therefore, with the question, "What am I going to do?"

The answer I came up with had to do with my sense of mission. I was here to test myself, to get embedded—the term Americans use since the war in Iraq started—in a foreign culture and see what happens. Without clear, accessible advice from an expert, I decided to rely on my intuition and poured the Pepsi over the ice.

I arrived back at the Riverside B&B at 7:00 and calculated that I had three hours left till bed time and really nothing to do. I thought about my time at *Wat Chiang Man* for awhile and then decided to get back into my murder mystery, *Bangkok Eight*. . . .and wait to see what my digestive system would do.

I got to a part where Detective Sonchai Jitpleecheep is reflecting on a conversation about cultural differences he is having with the blond FBI agent, Kimberly Jones. Sonchai muses, "The truth about human life is that for most of the time there is nothing to do and therefore the wise man—or woman—cultivates the art of doing nothing."

"A nice theory," I thought, "but in my life I rarely have nothing to do, and most of my friends complain about being stressed out, not bored."

As I read further, it's as if Detective Sonchai heard my objection. He states, "What I see is the great juggernaut of Western culture with its insane need to fill space, all of it, until there is no space or silence left."

There was no TV in the room, and I was tired of reading, so I lay back on my pillow and let the day's events pass through my mind as if I were watching a movie. It was at the point where I was sitting under a shade tree at the temple that I drifted off.

Not only did I wake up the next morning feeling refreshed after a good night's sleep, I felt so good about what I had experienced on the previous day, that I repeated everything I had done all over again—same breakfast, email, *tuk tuk*, *Wat Chiang Man*, hang out, pray, take pictures, *tuk tuk* and mom and pop restaurant.

The only difference was that I picked up a cold can of Coke from the 7 Eleven on the way to dinner. Maybe I had just gotten lucky yesterday.

13

Wat U Mong Thera Jan

Even though I've been to Thailand many times and should know better, I hang on to this fantasy that a real Buddhist monk is a skinny guy living in a hut by himself in the woods, dressed in a loin cloth and meditating all day.

I liked visiting the *wats* in Chiang Mai, but I felt that I somehow wasn't getting the real thing. So, when I read in my *Lonely Planet* guide book about the forest monks at *Wat U Mong*, I immediately decided I had to go there.

The day after my second visit to *Wat Chiang Man*, therefore, I crawled into a *tuk tuk* and asked the driver to go to *Wat U Mong Thera Jan*. When he finally understood where I wanted to go, he raised his eyebrows as if to say, "Do you realize that it's a good 45 minute ride from here and the ride is going to cost 300 baht?"

I let him know that I understood that the temple was way on the other side of town and that I wanted him to stay for the two hours I would be snooping around there, so he could take me back to the guest house. That brought a smile to his face, because making that much with one fare is a lot of money for a *tuk tuk* driver.

Immediately upon entering the gate to the forest temple, I felt like I had found what I was looking for. This wasn't just a little park in the city, but a large, what we would call in Chicago, forest preserve. Hundreds of acres of woods and trails on the outskirts of Chiang Mai.

No urban sounds were able to penetrate the insulation provided by the trees. *Lonely Planet* had called the setting *sylvan*, and so it was.

The *wihans* and *kutis* and the one *chedi* were restrained in their decoration and blended in with the natural environment. One lane led down a hill to a pond where ducks were feeding. As if to accentuate the importance of solitude, *Wat U Mong* is famous for a network of caves for meditating which had been dug into the side of the hill on which the understated *chedi* stands.

Buddha statue at Wat U Mong Thera Jahn

After looking around for ten minutes and absorbing the peaceful solitude, I wished I had more than two hours to just soak up the serenity of the place.

As I did my penguin waddle around the grounds I reached in my pocket to check and see if my purse was still there. It was something I did maybe twenty times a day. Just checking to make sure.

In an instant panic took the place of serenity. My pocket was empty. I checked my other pocket and then my back pack. My passport was safe in the money belt I wore inside my shirt, but my purse had my credit cards, health insurance cards and my driver's license, in addition to a couple thousand baht.

I felt weak. I tried to mentally retrace my steps. Had it fallen out while I was walking? No, it couldn't have. It had been down inside a deep pocket. Had I left the purse at the guesthouse? No, I don't think so? Maybe. . .I hope. . .maybe it had fallen out in the *tuk tuk* and when the driver would meet in an hour I would find it on the floor of the little taxi.

But that was an hour away, and there seemed to be nothing I could do in the meantime to relieve my panic.

OK, here I was in a Buddhist temple complex in the woods so it what be fitting, as I had done several times already on this adventure, to ask, "What would the Buddha do?"

I decided, as I usually did after asking that question, that he would begin by telling me to calm down, to take a few deep breathes and pay attention to my normal breathing after that. And then I decided that he would use the loss of my purse as a teaching moment to remind me that all things are impermanent, that the cause of suffering is getting attached to things.

Paying attention to my breathing did calm me down enough that the emotional paralysis I was feeling loosened up and I was able to think a little bit more rationally. I talked to myself. "What would the worst case scenario be? I guess it would be that I would have to call the credit card companies and tell them what had happened." I still had my passport, and I was sure that Sanit would float me a loan to pay for my expenses.

Being able to think things through helped reduce the panic a bit more, but it didn't come close to taking it away. While thinking about what the Buddha would say, I naturally was also thinking about what Jesus would say.

I had decided that my Bible reading during my time alone would be in the Gospel of Matthew. I had gotten into that sixth chapter that morning where, in the Sermon on the Mount, Jesus tells his followers to not be anxious. He says that the birds don't have jobs, but the Father feeds them; that the flowers don't work at all but they are clothed more beautiful than royalty in their finery.

So, was Jesus asking me to more or less "let go and let God," to not worry and trust that somehow everything would work out alright, to believe that God will provide? I felt embarrassed to consider praying for a divine intervention at that point when, just a few minutes ago, I had felt like I had everything under control.......but I prayed anyway.

All these things helped take the edge off, but the panic remained. Was there nothing I could do to fix the situation, or did I just have to live with my distress and wait for my *tuk tuk* driver to return?

It was then that I thought of some of my friends in Alcoholics Anonymous. AA has hundreds of little aphorisms or mantras designed to help people in recovery get through each day one day at a time. One of these is, "Fake it till you make it."

"OK," I said to myself, "behave as if you feel serene even though you are worried sick and feel powerless to do anything about it."

I started taking pictures. Then, when I saw a monk who looked like a Westerner, I asked him, "Do you speak English?" Turns out he was French and had been at this monastery for just a year, but, yes, he did speak English.

"Can you tell me where I can find a monk who has time to talk to me in English?" I had already decided that I was going to return soon and stay for the whole day.

He pointed to the lane leading to the pond and said someone would be there later that afternoon. I thanked him, but before we parted he asked me, "Are you alone?"

After I replied that I was in fact by myself, he said, "You have a lot of courage."

I didn't know what to say at first. *Courageous* is not a word I

61

would use to describe myself, so I felt like I needed to kind of deflect his statement, to explain what was really going on. I said, "I walk very slowly, but if I take my time, I'm usually OK." Then, as an afterthought, I added, "I probably see more that way."

He then made another statement that caught me as off guard as had his first comment. "I see that you are a teacher," he said.

Before I could respond, out of the corner of my eye I saw my *tuk tuk* driver running towards me, waving my purse in his hand.

14

Pondering and Muay Thai

When I saw my *tuk tuk* driver running toward me waving my purse in the air at *Wat U Mong*, my emotions instantly switched from panic to immense gratitude. The gratitude persisted through the evening and into the next morning.

It was troubling for me to admit to myself that I didn't feel this thankful very often. You know, living in the richest nation on earth, beneficiary of a great education, blessed with friends and meaningful work, etc., etc. All this and I still wake up grumpy half of the time.

I needed, I decided, to spend the whole day pondering. So after breakfast at the Riverside guest house, I walked down *Thanon Chiang Mai Lamphun* half a block, ordered an iced coffee at the Motto Coffee Shop, sat myself down on their small front porch and proceeded to try to digest what had happened to me the previous day.

I wasn't thinking really. This was getting to be a habit. My mind would often wander aimlessly. Most people, I suspect, wouldn't call it praying. What I needed to do was to let the emotion which had built up inside me percolate down into my soul. Percolating. . . . .pondering takes time.

The previous day had been an emotional roller coaster ride. Contentment in the forest monastery. Panic when I realized that I had lost my purse. Tremendous gratitude when it came back to me.

I pictured one of those forest monks telling me that they

never get into a panic about losing something, because they don't own anything. Nothing, but three sets of robes and their alms bowl. Everything is impermanent, they would explain. If you want to be at peace, cling to nothing.

But, I did cling to my purse. I prayed, not to let it go but to get it back. And, my prayer was answered. At least it was from my point of view, but I hesitate before I say that to anyone. I hesitate, because on the one hand one of my best friends back in Chicago is an agnostic. He doesn't see God's hand in anything, because he views reality through a different lens than I do. When I see a miracle, he sees good luck, and no amount of reasoning can change the fact that we see different things even though we are looking at the same phenomenon.

I hesitate, because on the other hand my evangelical friends are too confident, in my opinion, in their ability to KNOW what is from God and what is not. A pastor I know once quipped that graduates from evangelical schools KNOW that they are right, while alumni from Lutheran colleges HOPE they are right. I, clearly, am a graduate of a Lutheran college.

Part of my own "agnosticism," if you will, comes from a long list of what seemed to me for a long time to be unanswered prayers. I had prayed intensely for a month that my fifty year old father would recover from surgery. He died. I had prayed unceasingly that my marriages would get healthier. They both ended in divorce. I had prayed every morning for 24 years that my ministry would bear fruit. The congregation closed. I had hands laid on me ten, maybe fifteen times in the hope that I would be healed of my neurological disorder. It keeps getting worse.

Anne Lamott talks about her "consignment store faith" this way: "I know that when I call out, God will be near, and hear, and help eventually. Of course, it is the 'eventually' that throws one into despair." (*Grace (Eventually), Thoughts On Faith, p. 18*)

What I have is a consignment store faith. It's not pretty. It doesn't KNOW anything. It tries to trust but never quite gets there. It's not very much like Daniel in the lions' den. It's more like the guy who asked Jesus for healing, and when Jesus asked him if he believed he, ie Jesus, could do it, the man replied, "I believe. Help my unbelief." I've lived long enough with this faith of mine to believe that God answered my prayer the day before at *Wat U Mong*, but I would never be willing to say to a skeptic that I know that for sure.

I pondered and percolated and read some from the Bible and drank iced coffee there on the porch across the road from the Ping River in Chiang Mai for most of the day. Maybe it was because I wasn't sitting under a bodhi tree, but I never did achieve anything approaching enlightenment regarding what had happened to me the day before.

What I did know as the evening shadows lengthened was that I had gotten my fill of pondering for that day and was hungry for some dinner. I walked to the mom and pop open air restaurant in the corner of the parking lot and ordered a bowl of pad Thai with shrimp. After that I caught a *tuk tuk*, got dropped off at the boxing stadium near the Thapai Gate in the old part of Chiang Mai and had a wonderful evening watching three *Muay Thai* matches until midnight.

15

FACED WITH MY LIMITATIONS AT WAT CHEDI LUANG

I woke up on New Year's Eve morning trying to remember why I had decided to spend 40 days alone in Thailand. I recalled that I had imagined a time of testing, sort of like when Jesus was in the wilderness for 40 days and was tempted by the devil or when Israel was in the desert for 40 years and their faith was tested.

For whatever the reason, the first two weeks weren't at all like that. No demons. No temptations. Whenever I got into situations which were beyond my control, someone—Nicky, my *tuk tuk* driver or perfect strangers—came to my rescue.

I thought about the forest monk telling me that I had courage. He might have thought so, but the truth was that as long as I stayed in Chiang Mai, I had a safety net which was only a cell phone call away. Besides, it wasn't courage that propelled me but a kind of interior compulsion. I just had to do it. According to St. Mark's account, the Spirit "drove" Jesus out into the wilderness.

So, I decided to do what I had been considering for several days. Come Monday, I would strike out on my own on an eight day excursion to four smaller towns in this northern part of Thailand, travelling by train and by bus. Maybe then, hours away from help from my friends, the demons and dangers I had been expecting would appear to test me. At the very least, I would be able to explore some new towns and see some beautiful countryside.

Since the front desk of the Riverside B&B was also a travel agency, the women who staffed it helped me make guest house reservations in Lampang, Phayao, Chiang Rai and Nan. That settled, I addressed another unmet expectation.

Aside from my conversation in Bangkok's train station with Bikkhu Buddha Dhatu, I hadn't actually talked to any real Buddhist monks. I knew that a college was connected with *Wat Chedi Luang* and that the monks who were majoring in English would hang out in one part of the *wat* and strike up conversations with *farang* (Westerners) in order to improve their conversation skills.

After a short twenty minute ride in a *tuk tuk* I was at the *wat* and taking pictures. I remembered that the monks came to the *Monk Chat* area in the afternoon so, since it was still morning, I wandered around doing the things I always did in *wats*—read my Bible a little, hang out in the shade, let my mind wander, wait for surprises....

After awhile I noticed that I was feeling tired, because I had gotten to bed late after watching the *muay* Thai boxing match the night before. I was hungry, too, and hot, and I had to find a *hawng nam* (bathroom, literally water room). I left the shade of the big tree under which I was sitting and ventured into the hot sun almost directly over head, making my way around the ancient *chedi* in the middle of the *wat*.

The Chedi at Wat Chedi Luang

I was trying to be careful. I always try to walk carefully, because I trip and fall twice a month on average. It's because my disorder makes my leg muscles stiff and my balance bad. Most of my falls are what I call "good falls," i.e. nothing broken, no trip to the emergency room for stitches. I was trying to be careful, but all of a sudden there I was prone on the paving stones with the wind knocked out of me and a nasty scrape on my left forearm.

I was immediately surrounded by Thais asking me if I was OK. . . .at least I think that's what they were asking. They helped me get up and got me to a bench in the shade. After assuring them that I was not going to die, I was alone again.

It only took me a minute or two to figure out why I had fallen this time. I was tired, hot and hungry. I should have eaten a couple of granola bars before walking around the *chedi* to the monk chat. I sat for awhile, ate what I had in my back pack and very deliberately made my way to the shady spot where several college age monks were waiting for *farang* to talk to.

"Monk Chai" at Wat Chedi Luang

I spotted an empty seat at the little table where a *farang* couple was talking to a young monk. Turns out that they were from Switzerland. When I tried to enter into the conversation, the monk had a hard time understanding what I was saying. My resolve to venture out on my own was beginning to slip. First I fall down while trying to walk. Then I can't be understood while trying to talk.

Luckily, the two Swiss spoke excellent English and were able to "translate" my slurred speech into a language the monk could understand. When I thought about it later on, it was kind of funny—a young couple from the German speaking part of Switzerland helping me communicate in English with a Thai Monk—but at the time it felt like the changes and chances of life were confirming to me that I was disabled. So much for having courage.

After twenty minutes of telling each other where we grew up and how we liked being in Chiang Mai, we did finally get into the discussion I had been hoping for. I asked the monk, through my translators, to explain the concept of *kamma* to me. He talked about cause and effect—if you do good, you receive good, and vice versa.

"Ok," I thought, "he's saying the same thing I've heard before, so I think I understand at least one Buddhist concept." Having that little exchange go well motivated me to try to explain the Christian concept of *grace* to him. But, no matter how hard I tried, nothing I said, even when translated by the Swiss couple, seemed to make any sense to him. I tried saying it was an uncaused effect. Then I used the word *random* and then the word *surprise*, but nothing I said seemed plausible to him.

I left *Wat Chedi Luang* feeling chastised, grateful and grumpy all at the same time. When the *tuk tuk* crossed the Ping River I asked him to drop me off at the parking lot where the mom and pop restaurant was located instead of at the guest house. I ate a bowl of *lard nar*, picked up a taro filled dessert waffle from a vendor, ate it as I waddled the two blocks back to the Riverside B&B, and was in bed on New Year's Eve by 10:00 pm.

It had been a long day. I had been tested, not by demons or Satan, but by my own limitations. I was so tired that I didn't have the energy to try to process everything that had happened that day. I slept so soundly that I only half heard the fireworks being shot off at midnight.

16

Forest Monks, Thomas Merton and a Chicken

I would usually spend New Years Day with my son or daughter and friends watching the bowl games on TV and eating way too much food with empty calories. That not being possible in Chiang Mai, I decided to return to the forest monks who lived in *Wat U Mong Thera Jan* and spend the day there.

My *tuk tuk* driver dropped me off at the *wat* at 11:00 am and agreed to pick me up at 5:00 pm. I was ready for a quiet day. I was also ready to try getting into meditation. I had learned a little bit here and there about meditation during the years when I had been a pastor: sit in a comfortable position with feet on the floor; close your eyes; relax your jaw; relax your shoulders; pay attention to your breathing; imagine yourself in a garden. . . . .

But I wanted to learn more. The problem was that the classes on meditation offered by the forest monks in English were scheduled at times when I wouldn't be around, so I decided to try to get into it on my own.

After crawling out of the *tuk tuk* I headed towards a gazebo which was set on the side of a hill and overlooked a few *kutis* (monks' quarters), two life size Buddha statues and the pond. The scene felt peaceful, even romantic.

I found a comfortable spot on a bench, read my Bible, said my morning prayers, and watched a father show his daughter how to bow in front of the Buddha and plant incense sticks at the statue's feet. It was all very pleasant, but after half an hour I realized that whatever it was I was doing was not meditation.

Buddha Statue at Wat U Mong Thera Jan

I spotted a kiosk a short way from my gazebo with some books for sale. Since I had been unable on my last visit to *Wat U Mong* to find an English speaking monk and since I couldn't attend classes on meditation, I approached the kiosk hoping to find a book which would help me learn about the practice.

Sure enough. In the midst of several volumes in Thai, I found one thin book by Dr. Phramaha Chanya Khongchinda entitled *Introduction to Buddhism*. Since the author was from *Wat U Mong*, I hoped it would contain at least a chapter on meditation. I dropped 30 baht (about a dollar) into the coin box, took Khongchinda back to the gazebo and started reading.

To my disappointment, the monk had written nothing about meditating. Instead, I read a lot about rules, precepts, duties and virtues. He did touch on the core Buddhist understanding that the main problem in life is suffering and that suffering is caused by craving and attachment. "OK," I thought, "but I want to hear how a Buddhist tries to get rid of craving and attachments."

I had been sitting in my gazebo for an hour and a half, and this meditation thing was not working. On top of that I kept getting distracted by groups of Thai visitors strolling down the hill towards the pond on the lane which passed close by where I was seated.

Thinking I would find more solitude in another part of the *wat*, I put Khongchinda in my back pack, waddled up the hill to a spot in the forest where I seemed to be alone, sat down on a bench and tried again to meditate. Being finally alone felt good. The only sounds disturbing the silence were natural: a breeze rustling leaves, a bird chirping in the branches above me, the barking of an unseen dog.

It was then that I noticed the monk walking slowly towards me on one of the paths in the forest. I couldn't tell if his eyes were closed, but he seemed to be walking in a dream. When he got about a stone's throw from me, he slowly turned and began walking back in the direction from which he had come. Then, about thirty meters into the woods, he turned again and started back towards where I was sitting.

Back and forth the man with a shaved head and saffron colored robes walked. Going nowhere. I watched the monk for a long time. There was something calming about his unhurried, deliberate gait. I realized that I was beginning to envy him. The peaceful setting. Nothing to lose. No stress, No disappointments.

I wondered what he was thinking. . . .or not thinking. Was he trying to let go of craving and attachments? Or was he not trying to do anything, to kind of let go of everything? To just be?

Walking Meditation at Wat U Mong

He made me think of another monk, a Catholic named Thomas Merton who, as a Trappist, spent much of his day in silence. Over the years, Merton discovered that he had a lot in common with Buddhist monks like the one I was watching. Although their formulations of the nature of ultimate reality differed widely, their practice—the way they tried to connect with that ultimate reality—was very similar.

Merton died while attending a conference on meditation in Bangkok which was attended by both Christians and Buddhists. On the way to Thailand he was able to have three visits with the Dalai Lama.

About the visits Merton wrote, "It was a very warm and cordial discussion and at the end I felt we had become very good friends and were somehow quite close to one another. I feel a great respect and fondness for him as a person and believe, too, that there is a real spiritual bond between us. He remarked that I was a 'Catholic *geshe*,' which Harold [a companion] said, was the highest possible praise from a *Gelugpa*, like an honorary doctorate!" ("Asian Journal," pgs. 124-125)."

In his essay, *The Thomas Merton Connection: What Was the Christian Monk Looking to Find in His Dialogue with Buddhism?*, Alan Altany wrote,

> Being so deeply infused with his own spiritual tradition was what really allowed him to, paradoxically, appreciate people in other religions also so rooted and to appreciate their traditions, as from the inside--as vehicles of truth-telling and enlightening experience. Thus, religious dialogue for Merton was not a syncretism or an eclectic accumulation that ignored real differences in an attempt to create a universal religion (without specific roots).

I have felt the same closeness several times in my life with people whose understanding of the nature of ultimate reality differed widely from mine—a rabbi, an agnostic, a Mormon, a forest monk doing walking meditation.

Thinking about Merton made me recall something I had just heard in the gazebo from Khongchinda, who at the moment was still in my back pack. He had written, "The important issue which one should conceive is that Buddhism is not metaphysical but practical in our daily life and in every movement of living."

Not metaphysical. Indeed, a Zen master I knew back in Chicago had once told me that Buddhism is a non-theistic religion. God, if he or she exists, is irrelevant. He even added that some people think of Buddhism more as a psychology than a religion. I began to wonder if my fascination with this Eastern "religion" was not, as I had feared at times, a betrayal of my faith in Jesus Christ.

It was then that I remembered an experience I had a few weeks before while still on the mission encounter tour I was helping to lead. We were in Laos at a place called *Buddha Park*. As we wandered around the grounds, I watched an Evangelical pastor ask the group of people with him to all lay their hands on a Buddha statue as he prayed, "Lord, we ask you to rid this land of this evil, this idolatry which is keeping this people in bondage."

I couldn't pray that prayer with him. Not in my heart. The Evangelical point of view which he and most of the members of the group had caused them to consider the Bible's truth to be inerrant. You had to accept Jesus in your heart to be saved. If you're not for Christ, you're against him. Most thinkers in the field of world religions would label this point of view *Exclusivism*, i.e. my religion has a lock on ultimate truth and you need to convert in order to be saved.

I saw a lot more ambiguity in life than they did. To me, that forest monk doing his walking meditation just didn't seem to be a manifestation of evil.

As I looked up from my ponderings, I realized that the monk was no longer on the path. No longer having him to focus my musing on, I shifted my attention to a rustling sound to my left. I turned and saw a hen scratching in the leaves, exposing the ground underneath so that her ten chicks could peck around and find food.

She did this several times and then, scratching out a hollow in the leaves and the dirt, she gathered her large family under her. I'm not sure what raised the alarm in her. Maybe she noticed me and became frightened. Maybe she did this every once in awhile, like the Japanese who live in coastal towns do tsunami drills, just to stay in practice.

I couldn't get into that mother chicken's mind any more than I could discern what the meditating monk was thinking or not thinking. What I did figure out was that the hen and the monk were reading from different pages if not different books.

The hen was fiercely attached to her children, while Buddhists try to let go of attachments and cravings. It made me think of the time Jesus compared himself to a hen. He lamented that many times he, like a mother chicken, wanted to gather his children under the protection of his wings, but people wouldn't let him.

It was one more occasion for me to disagree with my monk friend whom I had met in the train station in Bangkok. All religions are not the same. Blurring the conceptual boundaries between them might make people feel tolerant and accepting in the short run but, over the long haul it makes the search for a meaningful worldview and way of life more difficult.

Doctrines are like a map you can use to find your way in an unfamiliar land. The vendor who sells you an inaccurate map might be a nice guy who makes you feel good as you interact, but days or weeks later, when you're trying to find your way back home, the bad map he sold you can lead you further from where you want to go than closer.

I never did get to talk to that monk doing his walking meditation on a forest path at *Wat U Mong*. The paradox is that although he and I would be light years apart in the way we would describe ultimate concerns—I confess Jesus Christ as my Lord and

Savior—I nevertheless felt a spiritual kinship with him.

I began to wonder. Maybe my forty days alone in Thailand were not going to be one confrontation with demons after another, but an opportunity to learn more about who I am by bumping up against a people, a culture and a religion which sees reality in a whole different light.

17

The Limits of Intimacy

and the Impact of Western Culture

Nicky and M picked me up at the Riverside B&B the day after New Year's Day, so I could worship with them at the *Nong Bua Sam* Church.

At the end of the service Sanit , as usual, asked me if I wanted to greet the congregation. Even though I'd been with them six times in the last two weeks, Thai courtesy demands that visitors be acknowledged.

I decided to try being funny. I did so with a little trepidation, because often in the past when I told jokes in multicultural settings, they had bombed. People from non-Western cultures just couldn't get my humor.

"I have a new name," I said and waited for Sanit to translate. Looking around at the faces of the *Nong Bua Sam* members, I knew that at least I had gotten their attention. "My new name is *Ajahn Cha Chaa.*"

It took most of the people sitting in the pews a few seconds to sift through my bad pronunciation, but when they finally understood, most smiled and I think two even laughed. "*Ajahn Cha Chaa*—Pastor Slowly," they kept repeating. The self-deprecating humor had worked!

I then told them that their church felt like a home away from home. I had been with them so many times since 1994 and had been welcomed with such generosity and respect that I really did feel that I belonged and was safe in this place and with these people. That made them smile again.

Likewise, as we were eating lunch together after the service, they all understood my frustration at not being able to explain the concept of grace to the monk at *Wat Chedi Luang*. I felt comfortable being with people who viewed life through the same set of theological lenses that I did.

My feeling at home with these people, however, was tempered by an awareness which had been growing in me for years that I didn't know one single Thai well on a personal level. I had been working with Thais back in Forest Park since they began sharing our church building in 1992, and had gone on retreats and overnight trips with many of them, yet I knew little or about their personal lives or feelings.

The language barrier was hard to overcome, of course, but increasingly I was coming to think that the cultural wall was even higher. Thai culture, for example, looks down on expressions of intense emotion. To answer the question "who am I," traditional Thais look not to self-expression and finding the "real me" but to their role in the family and their status in the social hierarchy.

Dr. Niels Mulder refers to this outward looking approach to personal identity as "social presentation." He writes,

> Whatever is behind the social presentation is secretive,
> for the other and for the person concerned. Presentation
> masks the latent whirlpool of emotions and drives.
> These should be left alone and out of sight: they may
> be explosive, threatening, and no good can come
> from them. (*Inside Thai Society, pp 90-91*)

To keep all of the internal psychological magma from erupting, Thais tend to cultivate a kind of self-mastery involving two concepts:

choei or remaining indifferent and *chaiyen*, maintaining a cool heart. (Mulder, pp. 89-91)

Whereas the primary criterion for judging a church or a family to be healthy for a Thai is the concern for everyone getting along by knowing their place in the social order, the American culture in which I am embedded keeps asking the questions, "can I be myself" and "is there closeness and even intimacy".

As my awareness of this tension increased—i.e. that I felt at home at *Nong Bua Sam* and at the same time was a *farang*, a foreigner--Sanit told me that a young woman nicknamed Oat would be driving me back to my guesthouse in town. I had noticed Oat during the service—cute as a bug's ear and looking to be about eighteen years old. Now, that's not saying much, because I find most Thai women to be attractive and much older than they look.

During the forty minute drive back to the Riverside B&B, Oat managed to smash some more of my generalizations about Thais. First, she let me know that she was a professor of psychology at a university in Chiang Rai, a couple hundred kilometers north of Chiang Mai. Her English was quite good, which helped the communication between us.

What I experienced, however, in a little more than half an hour was a Thai adult who was quite open with me about very personal matters. The daughter of a Christian pastor in Chiang Rai, she confessed to having questions about her relationship with God recently and that the sermon that day had been helpful. When I told her about my not feeling close to any Thai people, she talked freely about her own attempts at openness, intimacy and expression of emotion.

"Thailand is changing," she said. "Globalization has changed everything." Indeed, I remembered several occasions during this trip when I had seen young Thai couples holding hands as they walked down the street, something I never saw in 1994 when I first visited Thailand.

When she dropped me off at the guesthouse, she said that she had really enjoyed our conversation and gave me her professional card so we could stay in touch. As I waddled through the courtyard to my room I naturally felt good about being able to connect with an attractive Thai woman who was half my age.

It also impressed me how the new imperialism which the West brings to the East is not political but cultural. The means are not military action but the mass media.

All of this is for better and for worse. My son, who was an anthropology and archaeology major in college at the time, said that many scholars in his field are critical of Christian missionaries for intruding on a culture and trying to change it.

The irony of it all is that even though Protestant missionaries have been in Thailand since 1828, the country is still only 1% Christian. Yet, Western culture has managed to foment a cultural revolution in old Siam. Perfectly capable of resisting efforts to convert them to Christianity, Thais seem to be increasingly powerless against the onslaught of Western individualism and consumerism.

McDonalds and KFC are everywhere. Young professionals can be seen sipping cups of gourmet coffee as they negotiate the omnipresent traffic jams on their drive to workplaces in air conditioned high rise office buildings. One monk I was talking to mentioned that he was a fan of Manchester United. When I asked him how he knew about English soccer, he replied in good English, "Oh, I watch it on satellite TV."

Manchester United Soccer Fans

18

ALONE, BORED AND FRUSTRATED

I woke up the next day, Monday morning, feeling a mixture of anticipation and anxiety. This was the day I was going to set off on my eight day time of spiritual testing. I would get on the train in Chiang Mai at 9:00 am and ride for two hours to Lampang.

After two nights in Lampang, a bus to Phayao. One night there and another bus to Chiang Rai near the border with Myanmar. Two nights there and a bus to Nan. And finally a bus back to Chiang Mai after two days in Nan.

I had two goals in mind: 1) explore some small "charming" towns in northern Thailand I'd never been to before and 2) be much more alone than I had been in Chiang Mai, where a rather large safety net of people was always no more than half an hour away.

The adventure began well enough. The porters at the train station helped get me in the right car and found a seat for me in a section reserved for "monks, handicapped and the elderly." I had gotten to the train on time. Buying the ticket had gone smoothly. I learned that my car had a bathroom. My anxiety lessened and my anticipation grew.

We pulled out of the station only fifteen minutes late, which is "early" by Thai standards, and glided past rice fields and *lamyao* orchards. Many of the little country *wat*s we passed had chimneys, indicating the presence of crematories—something I never saw in the big cities. The charming scenery and the click clack of the wheels on the rails had a calming effect on me as we began to climb into the mountains.

It was fun watching the women who would get on the train in one town and walk through the cars selling bags of sticky rice, roasted chicken, cut up fruit and bottled water. They'd stay on the train for half an hour, selling their home made goodies, then get off the train and presumably catch the next train going back home.

I began to look forward to actually enjoying being with these kinds of salt of the earth people which I imagined would be living in Lampang, a town of 50,000 which the *Lonely Planet* described as being off the beaten tourist path and having an "undiscovered" feel to it.

Not only did Lampang have a lot of beautiful teak buildings—having been a center for the teak trade in northern Thailand—but was well known among Thais for having many horse drawn carts. In fact, Thais refer to the place as *Meuang Rot Mah*, i.e. Horse Cart City, because it's the only town in Thailand where horse carts are still used for public transportation.

About an hour into the train ride, we stopped at a little hamlet right in the middle of the mountains, and a group of ten teenagers carrying backpacks, smelling of smoke and holding liter bottles of Leo Beer climbed on board. Since all of the seats were filled by that time they sat on the floor, "camping" out right by my feet.

I began feeling not only alone but also very out of place. I usually feel insecure when I'm with adolescents, even when I'm back home. And even though none of them ever gave me a look which said "what is this old *farang* doing on our turf," I still felt—imagined is really a better word—like I didn't belong. That's what often happens in me. When I don't understand what people around me are saying, my imagination wants to fill the mental vacuum, usually with something fearful.

One of them started playing a beat up old guitar and some of the young people sang a few current pop tunes with him in Thai. He wasn't all that bad a musician, but I still felt great relief when they got off the train half an hour later.

The train arrived in Lampang two stops later. I got off, found a toilet, snacked on some cookies, got my bearings, and walked through the small train station and out the front door to find transportation to the guesthouse where I had reserved a room.

Three *sawng taeou* drivers stood nearby chatting, and one of them caught my eye. I said in *farang* Thai, "Pom bpai Riverside Guesthouse." The three drivers conferred and one said—or at least I think he said—"I know where it is. Hop in."

As I struggled to climb in the back of the red pick up with the two benches and a metal roof I said, "*Cha chaa* (slowly)."

"*Cha chaa,*" he repeated with a smile. We drove through the center of town, crossed the Mae Wang River, and after only a ten minute drive he dropped me off at the guesthouse. As advertised, the place was a large teak house reconfigured into small guest rooms. The floors were polished wood with a few cracks showing between boards which didn't fit together perfectly. No AC. No TV, but a hammock on the front porch which had a view of the Mae Wang taking its time flowing downstream. The place cost 250 baht ($9) a night.

So far, so good. Up till this point, the spiritual test hadn't been very difficult. Buoyed by a feeling that I knew what I was doing, I checked the pages on Lampang which I had cut out of the *Lonely Planet* and quickly decided that I would first explore *Wat Phra Kaew Don Tao* where the main *chedi* or *stupa* revealed a Hariphunchai influence. I had no idea what Hariphunchai meant, but it sounded cool. Maybe I'd even get to ride in a horse cart.

I approached the guest house owner who spoke English fairly well and told him my plan. He called a *sawng taeou* driver and in ten minutes I was at the Buddhist temple.

My first reaction as I looked around was, "So, what's the big deal?" This *wat* looks pretty much the same as all the others. Same components. Same colors. Same architecture. The only thing that was different was how the components were arranged.

Maybe I was getting spoiled. Like with Thai food and Thai women. When they arrive in Thailand for the first time, many visitors rave about the delicious food and—especially the men—comment on the beauty of Thai women. But, this was my seventh trip to the land of smiles. Was I in fact getting spoiled? "Oh, yes. Another delicious plate of *lard nar* served by an extremely attractive young woman in an open air restaurant adjacent to an exotic temple. So, what else is new?"

Or, was it something else?

I dutifully walked around the compound, finding a bench in the shade to sit on and rest every twenty minutes or so. I took pictures of the *chedi* and the *wihan* and the teak *kutis* where the monks lived, but I wasn't having much fun.

Teak Kuti in Lampang

What's more it's always an effort for me to walk—or more accurately waddle—around for any length of time. The stiffness in my legs makes them tire easily. On top of that I'm always worried about tripping and falling. The scrape on my arm from my fall at *Wat Chedi Luang* had not healed yet. The vigilance wears on me. Often during the day I pray, "Lord, please keep me from falling" and redouble my efforts to focus on what I'm doing.

Because I have to look at the ground to avoid cracks and roots I could trip over, I have to stop waddling every fifty feet or so, stand still and look up in order to see what is around me. As I proceeded from one shady spot near the monk's *kuti* to a bench under a tree next to the big *chedi*, I became aware of a man in his twenties watching me. As I approached the bench near which he was standing, he smiled as if he wanted to interact.

"Where you from?"

"America. Chicago."

"Ah, Chicago. Far away."

"Yes." I had to smile. The guy was trying hard to make a connection, and in a smaller town like Lampang, he didn't get many chances to practice his English."

"Are you alone?" It was the question several people had asked me already.

"Yes," I answered, wondering what his reaction would be.

"I admire you," he said, giving me a thumbs up.

It was nice to get an unsolicited affirmation. I continued to waddle around the *chedi*, taking frequent rest breaks on benches. Realizing that I was running out of gas, I headed for the entrance to the *wat* and waited for a *sawng taeou* to come by.

Within a few minutes I was able to flag one down. "*Pom bpai ran ahan One Alloi*," I told him, assuming that he would understand immediately. In Chiang Mai or Bangkok the taxi and *tuk tuk* drivers knew where all the restaurants were, but this guy just shook his head indicating that he had no idea what I was talking about.

I tried three more times. No understanding. I tried writing it out. "No read English. He said wait a minute and went to get reinforcements. The guy he brought back couldn't understand me either. "Geez," I thought, "it's just the name of a restaurant. My Thai can't be that bad."

By then a small crowd was gathering, and after hearing that this *farang* was trying to get somewhere but we can't understand him, everyone took a shot at figuring out what I wanted. It was déjà vu all over again.

Finally a woman came by who spoke English and understood what I wanted. When she explained in Thai what I was asking for, as had happened before, the crowd said in chorus, "Ran *ahan One Alloi.*"

And, as in the past, I muttered to myself, "That's what I said," knowing perfectly well that once again I had gotten the tones wrong and said something like I want to hit myself in the head with a brick. I also wondered how many cabbies in Chicago would spend fifteen minutes on a foreigner they couldn't understand.

Before I crawled in the back of the red pick up with two benches that would transport me to dinner, the woman who spoke English said, "You alone?"

"Yes."

Shaking her head in a disapproving way, she said, "You be careful." I never know how people are going to react to this handicapped guy out exploring on his own in a country where he is quite vulnerable. Some say I have courage, while others look at me as if I have no common sense.

I ate al fresco at One Alloi and tried to bounce back from a disappointing day. As the shadows lengthened I paid my bill and stood on the curb to flag down a *sawng taeou* to take me back to the guest house. Within in a couple minutes one pulled over and asked me where I wanted to go. This time I was prepared by having a business card with Riverside Guest House printed in Thai. He said OK and I crawled in the back of the truck *cha chaa.*

"Finally something is going smoothly," I thought as we crossed the *Mae Wang.* I knew we were headed in the right direction. But then, unexpectedly, the driver pulled over and showed a food vendor on the street the card and asked where the place was. He got back in, drove a few kilometers, pulled over and asked a man walking on the sidewalk for directions. At a third stop, the woman pointed down the *soi* we were on, and in two minutes I was "home."

I climbed the teak steps to the porch, unlocked my door, set my back pack down on the floor and flopped on the bed. Nothing terrible had happened that day, but I felt exhausted and at the same time bored.

$9 guesthouse room in Lampang

"I wish I had brought a novel along," I said to myself, realizing that I still had three hours left till bedtime and absolutely nothing to do. As I said earlier, before leaving for Thailand I had told my friends that often my only companions on my solitary adventure would be myself and God, and at that point I didn't find either one of them very interesting.

I would have hung out on the porch swinging in the hammock were it not for the mosquitoes which enforced a kind of house arrest every evening when the sun goes down a little after 6:00. I lay on the bed wondering how I could kill the next 180 minutes. I never thought of myself as a person who needs a lot of stimulation, but all I could think of was, "I wish I had brought a book along."

19

ALONE BUT NOT LONELY

I crawled out of bed at 9:00 am after sleeping for twelve hours. Boredom along with feeling slightly out of control can be exhausting.

Maybe feeling rested was enough motivation to make me take another shot at exploring Lampang. After a breakfast of soy milk and crackers, I asked the guest house to call for a *sawng taeou*.

"This one speaks English," he assured me.

I had learned something from the previous day's frustrations. Not only are there no *tuk tuks* in this small town, there aren't any *sawng taeous* or horse carts hanging around the Buddhist temples like in Bangkok and Chiang Mai. And, if a *sawng taeou* does come by, there's a good chance the driver won't speak English.

Today I would not only get a driver with whom I could communicate, but I would hire him for the whole day. When he arrived after only a few minutes, I asked him, "*Tao rai?*(how much?) for driving me to the teak mansion, a stop at a bank, *Wat Si Rong Meuang* and then the Riverside Bar for dinner?"

"600 baht," he replied.

"*Peng mak*(very expensive)," I blurted out.

"No, that's a fair price," the guest house owner said.

I knew on the one hand that 600 baht was equal to maybe $20 US. You can't get a cab in Chicago for half an hour at that price. On the other hand, I'd been taking taxis, *tuk tuks* and *sawng taeous* in Thailand since 1994, and that amount sounded exorbitant by Thai standards.

"OK," I replied after realizing that I didn't have many options.

Baan Sao Nak, a 100 old teak mansion once owned by a *khun ying* (aristocratic lady), was an interesting window into the lives of the privileged class in northern Thailand who grew wealthy from the teak trade a hundred years ago. I also saw my first horse carts parked outside, which was fun.

The next stop was Siam Commercial Bank where I intended to exchange a hundred dollars for baht. "*Sip natee* (ten minutes)," I told the driver and entered the bank's lobby. My turn came after five minutes and I handed over my debit card and the requisite passport before filling out the usual paper work. Five minutes passed. Then ten, and then twenty. I couldn't understand what the teller was saying to her supervisor.

Finally, after half an hour, someone who spoke English told me that their computer was down and asked if I could come back later. I wasn't surprised. I had experienced delays in Thailand caused by technological malfunctions many times before. *Irritated* is a better word. Why did they wait half an hour to tell me? This frustration was not part of my plans.

Responding to the puzzled look on my driver's face, I said simply, "Computer," and he nodded with understanding.

The next stop was the Burmese style Buddhist temple called *Wat Si Rong Meuang*. As my *sawng taeou* pulled inside the gate, my spirit lifted. This *wat* was different. There was still some construction going on in the main *wihan*, and I enjoyed watching the skilled artisans at work.

I asked the driver to stop at another bank after leaving the temple. This time I was in and out in ten minutes. A five minute ride through Lampang to the Mae Wang River and I was dropped off at the Riverside Bar with the understanding that my driver would return to get me at 7:00 pm. It was the middle of the afternoon.

Wat Si Rong Meuang in Lampang

The Riverside, like my guesthouse, is a beautiful teak building. On top of that, it has an open air dining area overlooking the *Mae Wang*. The place was empty except for two servers chatting at a table. I pointed to a spot by the wooden railing, and one of the servers nodded. I set my back pack on the floor, sat down and in a few minutes I was sipping the iced coffee I had ordered.

To my surprise, a feeling of well-being washed over me. Less than a day before I had been bored. This day had gone a little better than the day before, but there had been bumps on this day's road as well. For some reason the solitude today felt comfortable.

Maybe it was the ambience. The *Mae Wang* right below me meandering downstream. An occasional motorbike or car passing along the opposite bank but nothing like the traffic in the big cities. The trees and the *chedi* of a temple downriver reflected in the water. The clip clop of horses on the street outside. The chirping of a gecko. A place in the shade with a pleasant breeze.

Maybe it was that functioning in another culture is hard work—not knowing well the language, the subtle cues, the etiquette—

Riverside Bar on the Mae Wang

and that it was a relief to be away from the challenge and rest for awhile.

Or maybe it was just the natural ebb and flow of life. Sometimes I'm feeling up and sometimes I'm feeling down, and sometimes I can't figure out why. It, as they say, just is.

I opened the spiral stenographers notebook I was using as my journal and began to write. The images and stories, the emotions just poured out of me. In stark contrast to the night before, I wished that I had ten hours alone in this place instead of four.

Also unlike the night before, I found myself to be an interesting companion. Back and forth the conversation went between me and myself.

"Wasn't that temple interesting?"

"Can't wait to show pictures of it to friends back home."

"Why do you think we got so irritated when the bank employees took so long to tell us about the computer? We should know by now that that sort of things happens here."

"I'm not sure."

"What would the Buddha say?"

"What would Jesus do?"

Evening on the river at Mae Wang

The questions without easy answers weren't frustrating as I sat in the quietness of the Riverside Bar. I didn't need answers, because that day I felt like I was with two companions I loved and who loved me. In some ways, it didn't matter what we talked about. People falling in love often communicate without saying a word. My church sometimes calls relating like that *communion*. Martin Buber called it an *I-thou relationship*.

One translation of Luke's gospel says that after experiencing the conception and birth of Jesus, the flight to Egypt and the boyhood of Jesus, Mary *pondered* these things in her heart. No need to analyze. No urgency to figure them out. Simply turning them over and over in her mind, simply letting them soak into her spirit like a gentle spring rain percolates into the earth and adds to the aquifer deep below the surface.

I just let the feelings and impressions tumble out into the notebook, looking up frequently at the river, feeling the peacefulness, not wanting to be anywhere else in the world.

I have a daily devotions book at home called *Touchstones* (M.A.F., Hazelden). Several of the meditations in it are on solitude. Following are some quotes:

> Often it is not the events in our lives that bring change but the space between the events. (April 14)

> Spiritual progress is made by pushing aside busyness and efficiency. . . .We become receptive to inspiration, to a deeper wisdom, to that part of life which we do not command. (May 9)

> The message comes in our solitude, when our defenses against truth are set aside. It comes popping out without our planning it. Our solitude is a relationship with ourselves. . . .(July 20)

I thought back to my peaceful hours on Kampan's porch. Unlike yesterday, today's solitude produced a surge of well being in which I felt comfortable with myself as my companion. Not only was I content being with myself, but I also felt like the two men on the road to Emmaus who, after walking for hours with Jesus without recognizing him, suddenly realized who he was and that he had been with them all along.

On one day being alone can produce boredom. On another day loneliness. And on the next day deeper contact with myself and God.

> We cannot create profound stillness. We can allow it. We can move into it. We can receive it. Many of us have been frightened by such a stillness because we are not familiar with the spiritual moment. . . .It is contact with God. (March 19)

On this day, I had no need of a book to entertain me.

20

INCOGNITO ANGEL

I was so absorbed in journal writing in the open air dining room at the Riverside Bar in Lampang that at first I didn't see the man who sat down two tables away from me. It was when I looked up to take a sip of my iced coffee that I noticed him.

He was a *farang*, a Westerner like me, about forty years old. At first I didn't even feel like saying hello. I was enjoying my solitude. But he looked pleasant enough, and I started to feel like I should at least acknowledge that he was there. I decided to make contact.

"Have you been in Lampang long?"

He looked up from reading his *Lonely Planet* guidebook and smiled. "Just got here yesterday—my wife and daughter and I. Leaving tomorrow. Not much to see in Lampang."

"I know what you mean, although today the teak house and the Burmese style *wat* were interesting."

"How long will you be here?"

"Arrived yesterday and will leave tomorrow."

I asked him if this is the first time he had been in Lampang. He told me that he had travelled in Asia for a whole year before he was married, but hadn't been in this part of the country before. He introduced himself as Mark from Great Britain and invited me to sit at his table. We began a conversation which lasted an hour and a half.

I felt attracted to him from the start. He had been divorced when he was 31 and felt a need to explore the world and learn from it, he said. He had cashed in his savings—around $15,000 U.S.—and had purchased a one way ticket to Beijing in 2000. He had no destination in mind back then. The journey was the destination.

He told me about his year of travelling alone in China, Nepal, Thailand and that he had met a woman in Cambodia who was now his wife. Along the way he would bump into people who would tell him about a place which sounded interesting, so using a lot of charade like hand motions, he would find a bus which he thought was heading in the right direction.

Often, because of the difficulty with communicating, he would never get to where he wanted to go, he said, so he would think, "OK. Here is where I am, so what can I experience here?" He said that he had learned a lot by getting lost.

In his travels, he had met a lot of nineteen year olds who had flown to beach towns like Pattaya in Thailand and spent their whole time drinking and patronizing sex workers, never getting out and seeing the rest of Thailand or Cambodia or whatever country they had gone to for their holiday. That naturally led into comments about how travel can open your mind, that is if your mind is open enough to venture out into a foreign culture.

Then, looking at his watch, he said, "I'd better get going. My wife will be waking up from her nap."

After Mark left, I went back to my table and started writing furiously in my journal, trying to remember everything we had talked about and begin digesting it. I suppose that from his point a view, what had just happened was two guys passing the time in a small town in Thailand by swapping travel stories. For me, what had happened went much deeper. This man whom I had never met before and would never see again had given me a narrative I could live in.

The story he told me was in many ways my story as well as his. It felt like much of my life had been lived in a foreign country where I was constantly misunderstanding the directions, not picking up on the cues, being the one who "didn't speak the language." I had laid out big plans for where I wanted to go in my life's journey but often wound up far from my intended destination.

Sometimes I had felt stupid, incompetent at traveling this journey called life. At other times I felt like the people giving me directions were either lying or making them up to hide the fact that they didn't know how to get to where they wanted to go either.

Yet, time after time I, as my father would often say, "fell into a pile of manure and came out smelling like a rose." When Mark said that some of the best experiences in his journey came out of the times he had been lost, I felt my heart leap for joy. Without realizing the gift he was giving me, he was telling me my story in a way that I had never heard it told before.

That's the power a narrative can have. It doesn't reveal truth in terms of concepts to be understood, and it doesn't empower everyone all the time or in the same way when it does. Rather, a profound narrative creates a spiritual world in which hearers can actually live and thereby gain a kind of orientation which frees them to move forward on their journey of discovery.

I always had trouble understanding the Bible as a kind of religious *trip tic* in which the fastest, safest way to get from here to there was laid out clearly for everyone who took the time to read it carefully. Certainly, it contains a lot of commandments and directions which have in fact helped me along life's way at times.

But, when I hit walls in my life—those painful times which I neither understood nor felt I deserved—the rules felt to me like either lies or judgments or fantasies incapable of providing direction in my time of disorientation.

Instead, I had found comfort and a way forward in those great stories like the Exodus which, to those Israelites stumbling around in the desert, had felt I'm sure more like a punishment than a liberation. I was able to identify with those disciples who couldn't make themselves believe the women who told them that Jesus had risen. Those stories were my stories. I lived in them, and they lived in me.

The Greek word for angel in the New Testament is *angelos*, the root meaning of which is messenger. I'm sure Mark was not thinking of himself as an angel while he was telling me his story, but from my side of the conversation he was indeed a holy messenger giving me the gift of truth in the form of a good story. "Do not neglect to show hospitality to strangers," says the Letter to the Hebrews (13:2), "for thereby some have entertained angels unawares."

Those who are supposed to be able to understand the signs of the times say that one characteristic of the Post-Modern age we are living in is a disillusionment with reason's ability to figure everything out, a distrust of the capacity of science to free us from our existential predicament.

I am coming to believe that the Bible is at heart a Post-Modern document. More profound than the commandments and concepts are the stories which, as Quakers like to say, "speak to our condition" in different ways, at different times in our lives.

I looked up from my writing to watch the shadows lengthen and enjoy the reflections on the Wang River. Two single person racing shells came into my line of vision, moving at a leisurely pace. The rowers were not in a hurry. The long, slender craft added to the romantic effect of the scene.

I got to thinking, though, how hard it must be to turn those things around. That kind of craft is built for speed, not for maneuverability. Racing shells would be useless in whitewater. I was brought up to believe that my life would turn out well if I walked—or rowed--the straight and narrow. As my life unfolded, it was neither straight nor narrow. What my life required of me was maneuverability more than speed.

Mark's story was meaningful to me, I realized, because in part it was a metaphor for how to navigate through the changes and chances of life.

21

A Gentle Roller Coaster Ride in Phayao

I woke up as the sun was just peeking over the horizon, because the bus for Phayao, the next stop on my trip, would leave Lampang early in the morning.

I asked the owner of the Riverside to call the *sawng taeou*. As I waited by the gate, I remembered how, in my opinion, the driver had overcharged me the day before. I suspected that he and the guesthouse owner were colluding.

When he arrived, I asked him, "*Tao rai satahnee rot may?*"(How much do you charge to the bus station?)

"200 baht," he answered.

I hadn't planned on saying what came out of mouth next. "100 baht," I replied with a firmness and authority I had picked up from teaching school for three years. I think what happened is that this feeling of being taken advantage of had built up enough that I found myself taking a stand.

"125 baht," he said immediately.

"OK," I said as I crawled into the back of the red pick up. The ride only took ten minutes, confirming the rightness of my bargaining stand. "The turkeys," I kept thinking all the way to the bus station.

"Those turkeys were taking advantage of me the other day."

I thought about a woman on the mission trip I was helping to lead a month before who had said that she just couldn't make herself bargain at the night bazaar with these people who make so much less money than we Americans do. Bargaining to her was reducing their already low earnings.

I felt a twinge of guilt, but then I thought, "I didn't make the rules. They did. This is their game, not mine, and in their game they were exploiting me, and they knew it."

When we arrived at the bus station, I wound up giving the guy 150 baht. The amount of money wasn't the issue. I wasn't an *ugly American* imposing my values on them. They had been messing with me. What felt good was the realization that I was no longer a completely naïve rookie in this game of navigating through Thai culture. I had, after all, a little control of how things went on this adventure.

The four hour bus trip from Lampang to Phayao followed routes 1035 and 120 for 130 km in basically a northeasterly direction. We went through two small towns, Chae Hom and Wang Nuea, and passed thousands of rice paddies in the countryside. It was between the harvest and planting seasons, so many of the paddies were tan with stubble.

Some farmers could be seen turning the ground over in preparation for planting with a plow pulled by a water buffalo or more commonly by a two wheeled tractor. I allowed my western eyes to view the scenes as romantic—salt of the earth people working the land in harmony with nature and all of that. In my head I knew better. My reading of Thai stories had made it clear that rice farming was hard, back breaking work.

Phayao has a population of 21,000. The first two *Lonely Planet* guidebooks I had bought in years past didn't even mention it. That's what I wanted, a small town with few tourists and a taste of the "real Thailand."

I soon discovered why it hadn't been included in the travel books until recently. There wasn't much to see. And I thought Lampang was boring. I checked in at the Tharn Thong Hotel and paid my 170 baht ($6) bill up front. My room was a windowless cement box decorated by graduates of the Alcatraz school of home decorating. The shower had no hot water, which was not a surprise since several of the lower rent places I've stayed at had the same set up.

Since it was early afternoon, I had time to explore one wat before dinner. *Lonely Planet* said that *Wat Sri Khom Kham* was worth a visit, so I asked the young lady at the desk to get me a *tuk tuk*. What arrived was a 100 cc motor bike with a side car driven by a guy way older than me who spoke no English. Thankfully, I was able to communicate where I wanted to go. Even though he couldn't get his rig to go faster than 20 mph, it only took ten minutes to get from the hotel's side of town to the *wat*.

What I saw when the old guy dropped me off was a temple complex which looked like every other small town *wat* I'd ever seen. The one exception was that this one looked a little newer than most which meant it didn't have much character, and there were no shade trees to rest

Golden Buddha in Phayao

I had to admit that the forty foot tall golden Buddha in the *wihan* was impressive, but I'd seen larger. One nice thing was that none of the visitors to the temple were *farang*. All seemed to be Thai. I was getting a taste of the "real" Thailand, but so far it wasn't very interested.

After taking a picture of the gleaming golden statue, I poked around the *wihan* where, in a corner, I discovered some coin operated machines. Each one had the picture of an older monk printed on the direction panel. As I was trying to figure out what they were for, I saw a woman insert three ten baht coins in one of the gizmos and push a button.

Coin Operated Blessing Machines

As she knelt with her hands together in a prayerful *wai*, I heard a voice coming out of the machine in what sounded like a blessing. A minute later, the voice stopped, the woman stood up, *waied* again and left the *wihan*. "So this is the real Thailand," I muttered to myself. "I wonder what the Buddha would say about what I had just seen." I thought for a moment and remembered what Bhikkhu Buddha Dhatu, the monk I had talked to in the Bangkok train station, had said. He had been critical of the way many monks were behaving, not strictly following the 227 precepts they were supposed to observe.

In *The Truth Of The Messengers* he had written, "Many temples have become marketplaces where *Sangha* members sell prayer beads, images of the *Buddhas*...and even decorations for the altar at home."(p. 22)

I decided that I had had enough exploring for the day and walked out of the *wihan* to temple gate where I waited for a *tuk tuk*, or whatever you call that motorbike which had brought me here. After fifteen minutes, a police officer approached me and asked if I needed a ride. He spoke about as much English as I spoke Thai but that turned out to be enough. He ran across the street to a market and returned in five minutes followed another motor bike taxi.

I tried to make him understand that I wanted to go to *Ran Ahan Chuechan* which the *Lonely Planet* had recommended as a good place to eat. Nothing worked. Finally I said, "*Thanon Kwan Phayao*," the road on which the restaurant was located, and that rang a bell.

Turns out that *Thanon Kwan Phayao* is a miniature version of Lake Shore Drive in Chicago. Instead of running along Lake Michigan this *thanon* took us past Lake Phayao. No buildings spoiled the view along the side of the road by the water, while the inland side was lined with seafood restaurants for four blocks.

When we arrived at the end of restaurant row, I hadn't seen any sign of a place called *Chuechan*, so I had the driver let me off at the one across the road from where we were parked. My guide book said that the highlight of a day in Phayao was watching the sun set over the *kwan* with the mountains in the background. This one had a view, but the longer I sat there alone, the more a bad feeling grew inside me. I couldn't tell you why the place felt creepy. I just didn't like the feel of it.

I decided to move on and find another spot. What I really wanted, I realized, was a big glass of Thai iced coffee. After three blocks of waddling, I found Thawan Coffee and Restaurant. It looked more American than I would have liked, but it served the drink I wanted.

As I sat on the open air deck of the restaurant, I felt the same sense of solitude wash over me which I had experienced the day before at the Riverside Bar in Lampang. The best iced coffee I had tasted thus far on my trip didn't hurt anything. I wrote in my journal and watched the people at the other tables.

After awhile I realized that in the hour I had been there, I hadn't seen one *farang*, not one Westerner. The place had a *farang* ambience, but its patrons were young Thais. This, I figured out, was a part of the real Thailand, too—young educated Thais with cosmopolitan tastes, even in a small town like Phayao.

Sunset on the Kwan

The sunset was indeed spectacular, making the water on the *kwan* sparkle and giving the mountains in the background a golden aura. I wished that my friends back home were there to share it with me, but I didn't feel lonely.

I decided to head for the Tharn Thong Hotel at around 7:00 pm. The bus for Chiang Rai was leaving at 8:00 the next morning, so I wanted to get to bed early. I paid my bill, walked down the stairs to the street and waited. And waited. And waited. One man who spoke a little English shrugged his shoulders and said, "Phayao. Small town. No taxi."

At the half hour mark, most of the feeling of well being that I had felt just thirty minutes earlier had evaporated. "OK. OK," I thought. "What would the Buddha do?"

"Detach and keep a cool heart," was the answer I heard inside my head.

"And what would Jesus do?" I asked myself next.

"Believe that the Father hears your prayer and will take care of you," was the response.

Two very different approaches to the problem of anxiety. Could I somehow combine them? I tried to remain calm. I prayed for any kind of transportation back to my $6 a night concrete cell.

Just then a man, who had been hanging out on the sidewalk for fifteen minutes and watching this little drama play out, approached me and asked, "Where you stay?"

"Tharn Thong," I replied with what seemed to be the right tones because he immediately repeated what I had said.

"I take you," he said and pointed to his motorbike, sans side car.

The ride back took only five minutes, but the whole way I kept whispering, "Thank you."

I burned my ankle on the exhaust pipe as I struggled to get off, gave my Good Samaritan driver a hundred baht note which seemed to please him, and hobbled to my cell. I flopped on the bed and luxuriated for a few minutes in the feeling that I had made it back "home" safely. The day had been a gentle emotional roller coaster ride. The highs had not been intoxicating and the lows had never approached despair.

I thought about the guy who had just given me a lift to the Tharn Thong. My agnostic friend back home would call his offer "good luck." The way I looked at the world, it was an answer to prayer. The Buddha, I decided, would say that it really doesn't matter.

I thought about Thich Naht Hanh who, in one of his books, told a story about a group of Vietnamese boat people. As long as the overcrowded boat moved inside the harbor, it proceeded without a problem, but when the little boat got out into the swells of the open sea, it eventually swamped and sank. The Zen master concluded his story by saying that it wasn't the waves that swamped the boat. What made it sink was that the people inside panicked, causing their small craft to rock and ship water.

Waking up at midnight I realized that I had fallen asleep with my clothes on.

22

LEARNING TO LEARN IN CHIANG RAI

One advantage of having no hot water in my cement cell at the low cost Tharn Thong Hotel was that the cold shower early in morning brought me to alert consciousness quickly. As I walked out my door, an older guy with a motor bike seemed to be expecting me. We were at the bus station in five minutes.

The bus ride to Chiang Rai would take only two hours, and the cost was just 45 baht. That was the good news. The bad news was that this *rot may* did not have a bathroom. A lot of us old geezers have what's called OAB, i.e. over active bladder, so a bus trip for even two hours can be anxiety raising. I looked around and saw that I was the only *farang* on the bus. "Great," I thought. "Whose idea was it to go on this trip alone?"

I can't read Thai, but every few kilometers on the highways there are signs telling drivers how much further they have to go to the towns ahead. I knew that Chiang Rai was only 104 km from Phayao, so by seeing which signs were decreasing in distance at the rate of about 25 km per half hour, I could tell where I was.

The pressure started building at about the one hour mark. "What would the Buddha say," I thought. "I know. Breathing. That's it. Breathe in. Breathe out. Pay attention to your breathing and not to your bladder."

It helped. It really did, but mitigating a problem is not the same as eliminating (pun intended) it. I wish I could have explained to the driver my predicament earlier in the game and maybe he would've stopped at a gas station or something like that, but my Thai vocabulary just wasn't up to such a sophisticated task. With only 20 km to go, I knew I was going to either embarrass myself or explode, so I said to the driver, "*Hawng Nam* (bathroom)."

The guy looked at me as if to say, "We're almost there."

I shrugged.

So he pulled over to the side of the road. Thankfully, we were in the country. I climbed down the steps and did my business right alongside the bus. My cheeks were red and hot as I returned to my seat, but everyone averted their eyes and acted as if nothing out of the ordinary had happened. Shame is a big deal in Thailand, and since most Thais are very good hearted, shaming someone is one of the last things they want to do. There are some parts of Thai culture I just love.

The next twenty minutes were uneventful, and when I got off the bus in what is the northernmost town of any size in Thailand, I looked for transportation. I knew right away that Chiang Rai was a "big town" (62,000 actually) because there were both *tuk tuks* and *sawng taeous* waiting for passengers at the station. The *tuk tuk* driver charged me 60 baht for the ten minute ride to the City Home Guesthouse. I didn't feel like bargaining with the guy, since I didn't know how far away it was.

The City Home charged 200 baht ($7) a night. The good news was that there was a window in my room and the shower had hot water. The bad news was that the shower was down the hall. I was fine with the trade offs.

After getting settled in, I was ready for some exploring. I made a deal with a *tuk tuk* driver waiting on the street outside the guesthouse to take me to the hill tribe museum and two *wats* and then drop me off at a coffee house I had read about in my guidebook called *Doi Chang*. We agreed on the price of 400 baht and away we went.

The hill tribe museum was very interesting. I had been in Hmong villages several times and had visited the Lahu Bible School outside of Chiang Mai three times, but I hadn't realized there were so many tribes living in the mountains of Northern Thailand as well as in Myanmar (Burma), Laos, Cambodia and Viet Nam.

Seven major tribes—Karen, Hmong, Yao, Lisu, Lahu, Lawa and Akha—lived around Chiang Rai, and as many more could be found in other parts of Southeast Asia.

Once again my picture of the real Thailand was broadened. Ethnic Thais include about 80% of the country's 64 million citizens. About 14% are ethnic Chinese with the next biggest group consisting of all of the tribal people.

Next on my introductory tour of Chiang Rai were *Wat Phra Kaeo* and *Wat Singh*. As far as I was concerned, the only interesting thing about the wats was the extensive use of teak in some of the *wihans* and *kutis*. Otherwise I reacted with a feeling of "been there, done that."

My *tuk tuk* driver dropped me off finally at the *Doi Chang* coffee house, which turned out to be the most beautiful coffee shop I'd ever visited. *Beautiful*, of course, is not a word typically used to describe a coffee shop, but this one was. Just to enter the place, I had to walk through a shaded stone garden with ferns, flowers and a little waterfall. On the inside beautiful art hung on the walls, and beautiful pastry was displayed in cases under the counter.

I ordered an iced coffee, and as I looked around I realized that all of the coffee beans that were for sale were not only grown around Chiang Rai but were also fairly traded. That got my attention, because I had been buying fair trade coffee for our church from Equal Exchange for years.

Since it was getting close to dinner time, I decided to return to *Doi Chang* the next day and just hang out, write in my journal and buy some of their coffee to take back home with me.

Not knowing exactly where I was in the city, I flagged down a *sawng taeou* and said I wanted to go to the night bazaar. The driver understood! and I crawled into the back of the pickup. To my surprise we passed the City Home in just two blocks and just a block and a half after that the driver stopped at the night bazaar.

"The turkey," I thought for the second time in three days. "That *tuk tuk* driver earlier in the day had taken me for a ride, as they say. He knew the guest house was within walking distance, and he took this ignorant *farang* to the City Home via the long, long route."

That's a problem with travelers who fear being *ugly Americans*. We want so badly not to offend that we're vulnerable to being taken advantage of. . . . .until we learn the ropes. It had taken half a day for me to learn this particular rope. It impressed on me how vulnerable I was and at the same time that I could learn.

That's a lesson I've learned about venturing out in a foreign culture. You'll always, to one degree or another, be a learner. People who've lived in Thailand for twenty, thirty years tell me that they do OK, are accepted and even loved as long as they don't try to be Thai.

It requires a certain comfort with a relatively high degree of not being in control. Although I've let go of a lot of that desire during my seven trips to Thailand, I recognized that some of it was still there. That "need" to be on top of things, to know the ropes, to not feel like I'm in fifth grade again and always in the position of being the learner.

In the late 1990s I read a book by Thomas Hawkins entitled *The Learning Congregation* in which he argues that in a rapidly changing culture, churches don't just have to learn how the world has changed in order to survive and prosper; they have to learn how to learn, because the world we know is constantly changing.

For an institution which wants to speak with authority, it's hard to learn this kind of humility. It was sobering to figure out that one of my personal issues was also a major issue for the institution to which I had devoted my life.

Hawkins compared it to canoeing in whitewater. To get through a 100 meter stretch of rapids with rocks, huge rooster tail waves and turbulence, a canoeist can't plot a straight course and hope to survive. To get through whitewater the two canoeists—who are in the same boat, as it were--have to communicate constantly, change direction frequently and adapt to a new challenge about every five seconds.

I thought back to those racing shells I had seen move so elegantly and effortlessly up the Wang River when I was in Lampang. On calm water they can move with grace and dignity, but they wouldn't get ten meters down a class III rapids.

I never liked the fact that I always felt like a little kid when I was in Thailand, never understanding for sure what was going on and almost always needing some kind of help. In my better moments I realized that what I was experiencing in an acute way while stumbling around in Thai culture was more or less what almost everyone goes through in this rapidly changing world.

Many of my Thai friends along with books I've read have said that one problem with Thai education for the most part is that it is based on the model of the expert teacher lecturing and the students memorizing. Many Thais know how to play that game in order to get their degrees, but the perceptive ones learn what Hawkins was talking about in the rock and roll world of trial and error experience outside the classroom.

I crawled out of the *tuk tuk*, paid the driver and started to check out the mom and pop noodle stalls at the edge of the night bazaar. One way you can tell for sure that you are in an authentic Thai restaurant is if there are no menus in English. Should I take a chance?

I saw some crispy noodles in a plastic container next to the big wok on the propane gas burner which motivated me to take another risk. In my best Thai I asked if those noodles meant that they served this dish I love called *kao soi*—coconut curry broth with soft noodles, an assortment of vegetables I never could identify, small pieces of

111

chicken and those crunchy noodles on top.

They nodded yes. I sat down on a plastic stool, and in a few minutes I was feasting on *kao soi gai* and a bottle of Singha beer, all of which cost me $3.

Kao Soi in Chiang Rai

23

Meditating in Chiang Rai—
Life is Like a Tomato

I woke up the next morning, a Friday, feeling like a wanted to loaf all day. I took my time showering and saw that it was 11:00 am by the time I was ready to go.

The hill tribe museum I had been to the day before was located above a restaurant called *Cabbages and Condoms* which is operated by the Population and Community Development Association (PDA), based in Bangkok. As the name of the restaurant implies, PDA is active in promoting family planning especially, in the Chiang Rai area, among tribal people. I decided I'd go there for lunch and check out what PDA was doing.

I have to admit that I felt a bit self-conscious when I walked into the place. The fact that all of the art on the walls was made from rolled up condoms in bright colors didn't help. And, sure enough, my server was very attractive.

Cabbages and Condoms turned out to be a disappointment. My server seemed bored with her job and didn't engage in any interaction. My lunch was good but overpriced, which I expected from an NGO trying to raise funds, but I didn't learn a thing. Too bad, because it sounded like they were trying to good work, but the place didn't motivate me to give them my email address and become a supporter.

I went out to the street intending to flag down a *tuk tuk* or *sawng taeou.* Instead I bumped into a *samlohr* driver, who turned out to be the least expensive transportation in town. I was able to communicate with him that I wanted to go to the *Doi Chang* coffee house, but he didn't know where it was.

I had studied the map that morning and had a general sense of where I was and where I wanted to go, and, to my great joy, he seemed to catch the drift of what I was saying. I crawled into the back of the rickshaw, and he began pedaling. At most the trip was two kilometers long, but by the time we arrived at *Doi Chang*, the guy was sweating.

Samlohr Driver

"*Khap khun krup,*" I said as I *waied* my hard working driver.

"*Mai pen rai* (no problem/you're welcome)," he replied, reciprocating the *wai.*

It was 1:00 pm, and I had nothing planned for the rest of the afternoon but to hang out at *Doi Chang.* Strange. Even though I had had such good experiences with unscheduled time on Kampan's porch in Chiang Mai and on the banks of the Mae Wang at the Riverside Bar in Lampang, I still had to work hard at convincing myself that I shouldn't feel guilty about "wasting" a whole afternoon.

I ordered an iced coffee, of course, picked up a day old copy of the Bangkok Post and tried to find out what had been going in the world since I left the States on December 1. I had been living in a parallel universe and was out of touch.

That brought to mind a difference I had noticed between the younger monks and their older mentors. The young men in saffron who practiced their English at the Monk Chats in Chiang Mai laughed a lot and were curious about everything going on in the world. I remembered the young monk, who had come all the way from Katmandu to study English in Chiang Mai, who told me he was a Man U fan.

In contrast, the older monks always seemed to be living in a zone disconnected from the world I moved around in. They had no interest in whether Manchester United had won its last football match or not. Except for the monk in Bangkok's train station, older monks never greeted me, smiled at me or even acknowledged that I existed. They just seemed to glide through life, "lost" in a detached, altered consciousness.

The reality from which I was disconnected was not the same reality from which the older monks I had seen were detaching. Or, was it? Back home I would watch the News Hour almost every evening and had my car radio set to NPR. My friends and I would often get into political debates, passionate at times, as if what we thought was really going to make a difference in the world. During my solitary journey in Thailand, however, I seemed to care less about what was making the headlines back home.

Speaking of back home, I realized that I had been seeing a lot more *farang* in Chiang Rai than I had seen in Phayao or Lampang. That's because Chiang Rai is perhaps the trekker capital of Thailand. Absent were the Westerners who wanted nothing more than to be tourists. That is, they wanted to "dip" into Thai culture from the shallow end of the pool, always staying in reach of the comfort of a five star hotel which served American food and where the staff spoke good English.

These *farang* in Chiang Rai were mainly Caucasians in their twenties, wore quick drying synthetic pants and shirts purchased from outdoor gear stores like REI and, when not wearing their hiking boots, made slapping sounds on the pavement with their flip flops. They were lean and tanned and carried their forty pound packs from the bus station to the cheapest guest house in town with ease. They were about diving into Thai culture at the deep end.

From the perspective of my 63 year old, disabled body, they all seemed to be on the upside of the bell curve of life. Their whole life was about growing. They were constantly acquiring new knowledge, new experiences, increasing confidence in themselves.

In contrast, I was clearly on the downward slope of the curve. My life was way more than half over, and my body, much like my twelve year old Mazda, was still useable but not worth very much as a trade in. I didn't wear flip flops, because I would trip in them and had left my hiking boots at home. I wore what they called "sensible shoes."

As I sat in the pleasant ambience of *Doi Chang* and watched these beautiful, young trekkers pass by on the sidewalk outside, I surprised myself by not feeling envious of them. Maybe it was partly because I had been able to have adventures when I had been their age. I had lived in Puerto Rico for two years. I had canoed the Boundary Waters and the Quetico five times. I had hiked Isle Royale alone for five days. What the sight of those lean young folks triggered in me were good memories more than envy.

But, there was a more profound reason why I wasn't jealous of their mobility and energy. I had done a lot of letting go during the last decade of my life. I had made peace, or at least a cease fire agreement, with the reality that I was inexorably sliding down the slope called *aging*. I had come to the conclusion that because the slide was inevitable, all I would accomplish by trying to resist it would be to be to look and feel like a fool.

So I watched other crones and codgers whom I admired and tried to imitate them by learning how to slide with grace. They didn't dye their hair, have tummy tucks done or pretend that they liked hip hop. They loved it when younger people enjoyed chatting with them, but they weren't desperate to gain their approval. They liked being where they were in life.

I decided that life was like a tomato. It begins as a tiny seed and needs a lot of nurturing when it first sprouts. After getting a good start, a tomato grows like crazy from May until August. But then, when the dog days of summer hit, it stops growing. For the rest of its time in the garden until there comes a killing frost, what tomatoes do is ripen. They don't become larger. They become juicier. I liked the thought of becoming juicy.

I had had enough of introspection by 4:30 pm, partly because I was getting hungry. So, based on what I had learned about where I was the day before, I chose to waddle the two blocks to the City Home and then the block and a half to the night market.

In the middle of Chiang Rai's night market is a huge open air dining area with maybe fifty tables surrounded by food stalls. A server from the stall nearest where you are sitting takes your order while you enjoy being in the mild, seventy degree evening air. As I waited for a sampler plate of Northern Thai food, I enjoyed the music played by two guitarists performing on a stage thirty meters from me.

Akha woman

Waffle Vender

After a fun meal, I browsed the market and found an Akha woman selling hand sewn purses--or *man bags* as my daughter corrects me when I say I'm carrying a purse—for 200 baht($7) each. To my eye, they were beautiful and within my budget. I like bringing fabric items as gifts for friends back home, because cloth doesn't break when luggage is thrown around at the airport. I bought four.

On my way back to City Home, I was still a little hungry so I bought one of the popular little waffle desserts—this one filled with taro—for 15 baht from a street vendor.

24

Angels Watching Over Me in Nan

The next morning I walked with my small backpack of just ten pounds the block and a half to the bus station early in the morning. I asked an agent at the window for a ticket to Nan, the last small town on my eight day side trip from Chiang Mai. The man said the tickets to Nan were being sold right outside the bus.

I walked over on the platform to where the bus was parked and asked for a ticket all the way to Nan. The agent looked at her clipboard, looked up and said, "No ticket. All full."

I felt my heart sink. Hadn't even thought of the possibility of there being no room on the bus. What was I going to do? What would Buddha say? I tried to find a calm place inside me so I could sort out my options. What would Jesus do? I prayed.

The agent must have felt some empathy for me when she saw the crestfallen look on my face, because the next thing I knew, she was calling what sounded like a supervisor on the phone. When she finished the call, she looked up at me and said, "have one space," and pointed to a place on her seating chart.

I did remember to pray, "thank you," not just because I had gotten a seat, but because it was a seat all the way in the rear of the bus......right next to the bathroom!

It turned out to be a six hour trip, partly because the distance to Nan from Chiang Rai is 228 km but also because the bus, I swear, spent half of the trip grinding in first or second gear. The road—following routes 1020, 1021 and 1091—includes hundreds of mountain switchbacks. The views were spectacular.

Mountains in Thailand are jungle covered all the way to the top, unless they had been deforested by tribal people, as many were. These poor hill people were trying to scratch a living out of the slopes. The mountains felt more like the Appalachians than the Rockies.

Nan felt as small as its population, 24,000. There were no *tuk tuks* or *sawng taeous* waiting at the bus station. I approached one of the two *samlohrs* standing by. We agreed on a price, and after ten minutes of pedaling the "driver" let me off at the Nan Guesthouse nestled in the trees at the end of a short *soi*.

"Mr. Tom?" I nodded. "We've been expecting you," said a pretty young woman in excellent English. After I took my shoes off on the porch, she led me to a pleasant room at the end of the hall. She said, yes, they had a laundry service and that they had a little restaurant right across the *soi*.

I thanked her and took my time getting settled in. I was tired. It always amazed me how sitting on a bus or plane for six hours tires me out.

After dinner at restaurant in the center of town, I was still hungry--mainly for something sweet—so I waddled across the *soi* to the small restaurant across from the guesthouse. The owner was having dinner with her two partners, and, in typical Thai fashion, she pulled an empty chair over to their table and invited me to sit with them.

After chatting for awhile, I mentioned that I was still hungry and asked if they had any desserts in their café. The owner said that they had none, disappointed that she couldn't respond to my request. That itself would have made my day—a bright, pretty young woman wanting to take care of me.

She then brightened up. "They have banana *rotee* at the night market," she said.

"Oh," I exclaimed. "I love banana *rotee*. But. . .I don't think I can walk all the way to the market." What Thais call *rotee* are these crepe like deserts filled with sweetened condensed milk and banana or chocolate or both.

"No, no," she replied. "I'll get one for you." She jumped in her car and in five minutes was back with a styrofoam box containing the sweet dessert I love.

"How much was it?" I asked.

"On the house," she answered with another smile.

Nan guesthouse owners

The next morning I got up and asked the owner if she knew where a certain Christian church was located. She said she did and called a *samlohr*. The old guy pedaling away in front of me found the church. A man standing at the front door greeted me in English as I crawled out of the rickshaw. My friend Sanit had called him from Chiang Mai and had asked him to welcome me.

Even if I had someone to translate, which I did not, the sermon as usual would have been way too long for me. I'm amazed at the tolerance Thai people have for long winded speeches. Still, it was good to have a church to go to, and again as usual the members outdid themselves in welcoming me.

As most Christian churches I've been to are in the habit of doing, this congregation served a simple lunch after the service. I sat with ten seminary students from Chiang Mai who had travelled to Nan to nurture the relationship between their school and the church by singing during worship. At lunch I practiced my Thai on them and they practiced their English on me. We laughed through the whole meal at our mispronunciations.

Following the meal, the pastor dropped me off at the Nan National Museum, housed in the early 20th century palace of Nan's last two feudal lords, each with an impressive sounding name: Pha Jao Suriyapongpalidet and Jao Mahaphrom Surathada. When I asked the lady at the desk how much it cost to enter, she said that it was a free day.

After the museum, I decided to walk across the street to the relatively small *Wat Hua Khluang.* I took off my shoes and went inside the main *wihan*, mainly to get out of the tropical sun and get off my feet. I had already done, what for me, was a lot of walking at the museum. I was grateful to be alone. That this *wihan* was similar to thousands of others in Thailand didn't matter to me at that point. I wasn't looking for stimulation.

After resting in the welcome solitude for twenty minutes, I waddled outside to check out what the *Lonely Planet* called the *Lanna/Lan Xang* style *stupa* in back of the *wihan.* As I inched my way carefully over the uneven paving stones, I saw a monk across the *wat's* lawn sitting in a chair and reading a newspaper.

I resumed my penguin waddle, looking down to make sure I didn't trip. Ten meters later, I looked up while stopping to rest, and I saw the monk holding a plastic chair in one hand and motioning with the other to walk across the lawn and rest under a tree.

I had never had a monk help me before. Most of the older monks seemed to not even be aware of my presence. Hundreds of every day lay people had helped me cross streets, find a *sawng taeou* or give me directions. I had started to form a bias that monks lacked that virtue of compassion that the Buddha had talked so much about. But, here, one more of my generalizations was being proved wrong.

I rested in the shade for another twenty minutes, and since there really wasn't much to see at *Wat Hua Khluang*, I thanked the monk, *khap khun krup*, and began my two block trek to a kind of town square where I hoped to catch a *samlohr* back to the Nan Guest House.

As I approached the gate to the *wat*, a small black and white dog joined me and escorted me across the street. The little guy didn't say anything, of course, but he seemed to have the mission of getting me across the street. I reached the opposite sidewalk safely, and the dog kept trotting along with my waddle. While I stopped to take a picture of another temple across the street, he sat down and waited for me.

Guardian Angels in Nan

He followed me all the way to the busy intersection which I had to cross to get to the square. I won't say they he waved good bye to me as I moved across the street, but I did feel like we had formed something of a bond in that two block walk we had taken together.

When I entered the square, I spotted a little coffee kiosk which I couldn't resist. I ordered my coffee, and the cutest blonde—and I don't think she had colored her hair—young Thai woman smiled as she handed me my cold drink. Then she ran around the counter and helped me to one of the tables under umbrellas set out in the plaza. I tell you. There's no tonic like these omnipresent beautiful young Thai women to make a 63 year old feel thirty years younger.

After finishing my coffee, I went back into the kiosk and asked the blonde, who was now accompanied by another equally attractive coworker, where I could find a *samlohr*. Her response was to take out her mobile phone and start to make calls. "You sit table," she said while closing her phone. "*Samlohr* come soon." At this point both young women helped me back to the table.

Five minutes later, my transportation arrived, and as I crawled into the *samlohr*, I looked back toward the coffee kiosk and saw the two young women waving good bye to me with, of course, big smiles on their faces.

What would Buddha say? I'm pretty sure that he would tell me that since there are no exceptions to the law of cause and effect, I must have done several meritorious acts to have earned all the good things that had happened to me during the last two days.

Jesus, on the other hand, would talk, I think, about guardian angels and grace and God being like a mother hen who looks out for her vulnerable chicks.

25

Believing Is Seeing

After the *samlohr* driver dropped me off back at the Nan Guest House, I was tired from walking a lot but not sleepy. It was only 3:00 in the afternoon, so I found a chair on the porch and just sat in the pleasant late afternoon air for a long time. I suppose I was hoping to recapture the serenity I felt on Kampan's porch in Chiang Mai.

I'm not sure how old the pre-toddler was who caught my eye. His mother was holding his two hands from behind as he made exuberant attempts at walking. His walking was even worse than my waddling, but he was loving the learning process.

Toddler and Mom   *Art on guesthouse wall*

He had a big grin on his face as he made his five meter dashes across the small lobby before collapsing in a heap on the floor with a squeal. Ten seconds of catching his breath and he'd hold up his hands to his mother to try it again.

The little tike and I had some things in common. We both

had trouble walking and both of us fell a lot. His falls, however, didn't hurt as much as mine, because he had a lot shorter distance to fall and his body was a lot more limber than mine. So, when I'm out doing my penguin waddle, I'm constantly aware that with my next step I might trip, fall and hurt myself. Walking is no longer pleasurable in itself. It's something I have to do in order get where I want to go.

I was again reminded that a big part of aging or dealing with a disability involves letting go of abilities we used to have.

In contrast, the little fella I was watching found the process of learning to walk a joyful experience. He was acquiring abilities and seemed to never tire of the thrill of learning new skills. His mother got worn out before he did and sat down for a break.

Not having his "training wheels" anymore, he resorted to crawling, exploring every corner of the lobby. At one point, he crawled under a table. His mother, who had been watching his every move, realized that if he stood up, her child would bang his head on the underside of the table top. She got up from her chair, moved over to the table and held her hand above her son's head, so if he did stand up her hand would cushion his head as it approached the immoveable object directly above him.

For the second time in an hour, I thought of Jesus' reference to himself as a mother chicken who cares for and protects her little ones. But, then I got to thinking. Was that mom unintentionally cheating her son out of a chance to learn about reality? I mean, if the little guy would stand up without her protection, he'd experience pain for sure, but no permanent damage would be done, and he'd never forget the important lesson that when crawling under tables, always look up before you stand up.

As I was pondering what the Buddha would say about the mother's behavior, another guest named David joined me on the porch. Turns out the guy was about my age and had a U.S. passport but lived in Beijing with his Chinese wife. He presented an air of cosmopolitan sophistication. Several social classes above me, I figured.

To my surprise, he engaged me in a conversation, and after chatting for awhile, he asked me what caused my slurred speech and stiff gait. For some reason, I almost always enjoy talking about my neurological disorder, so I explained that it is something like ALS, Lou Gehrig's Disease, but is not fatal, and that I'd had symptoms for at least fifteen years.

He listened to my story intently, and when I had finished, he said, "You seem to be handling your misfortune very well. You aren't depressed and have a great attitude."

I had heard comments like David's often, so it didn't catch me without an answer I could have given him—a kind of talking point ready to hand out on cue. Nevertheless, I found myself thinking about his statement for a moment before responding, "I'm only in a good place now, because I've done my grief work."

When I saw him raise his eyebrows, I continued, "What I've learned is that you can't jump from a loss directly into a happy adjustment. The leaders of my divorce recovery group years ago kept telling us that the only way out of pain is through it. I think they're right. I'm not depressed now, partly because I allowed myself to feel depressed for awhile early on."

I was feeling pretty satisfied with my response to David until I heard the Buddha talking to me in the back of my mind. "You see what I mean? Attachments cause suffering. No exceptions to the rule. If you want to be finally free from suffering, you have to accept deep in your psyche that everything is impermanent and then detach. OK, you're feeling better right now, but you had to suffer to get where you are. And it's only a matter of time before you. . . ."

I thought about what I had just told David and the Buddha's critique of what I had said for a moment as we sat in silence on the porch and the shadows lengthened on the *soi*. Is it really true that it's better to have loved and lost than to never have loved at all?

I considered revising my statement to my new and impermanent friend but decided against it. Instead I suggested that the two of us and his wife go out to dinner together. Word of our plans made its way around the guest house quickly so that by the time we were ready to order, our little party had grown to six foreigners: a Norwegian man named Lars who had married a Thai and spent his winters in Thailand and summers in Norway, a French woman who had just spent two weeks in Myanmar, a guy from Canada, David's Chinese wife, David and me.

Assuming that all Norwegians are Lutherans, I made an attempt at connecting with Lars by saying that I, too, am a Lutheran. Contrary to my plans—once again—my statement triggered a five minute rant by Lars about how religion is to blame for all the evils in the world and that it's simply a means for the powerful to control the masses. He was an atheist, he said, but if he were to practice a religion it would be Buddhism. You never hear of Buddhists starting wars, he said in conclusion.

I could have lectured Lars on the history of wars between Thailand and Burma to the west and the Khmer kingdom to the east. I could have ticked off a long list of the good things for which Christian missionaries are responsible in Thailand like schools, hospitals and social service agencies, but I held my tongue.

When I was twenty years younger I would have felt like I had to respond to Lars' rant, to set him straight, to adjust his attitude. The reason I kept silent was not because I lacked confidence. I had earned a Doctor of Minister degree and had a lot of intellectual ammunition with which to assault him.

I didn't say anything, because this was one more example of how people see "reality" from the perspective of different world views or plausibility structures. It's why, for example, I tended to see the good things that happened to me earlier in the day as gifts from a loving Father, while the Buddhist monk I had talked to back in Bangkok's train station would say the good things were the result of my *kaama* (karma).

Lars' cynicism about religion made me think back to my futile attempts at explaining grace to those young monks at the monk chat at *Wat Chedi Luang*. I was taught that the dictum, *seeing is believing*, is true. More and more I have come to think that what we believe determines what we see.

I was taught to not judge other people until I had walked a mile in their shoes. That means, it seems to me, that the shoes you walk in shape how your eyes perceive what is real and what is an illusion, what is plausible and what is not. So, if I want Buddhists to understand grace, how do I bridge the psycho/social/cultural gap and give them the experience of walking in my Western shoes, of viewing reality through biblical lenses? Especially, if that's the last thing they want to do?

26

Thai Women

The *samlohr* arrived at the Nan Guest House at 7:30 am to take me to the bus station. The bus ride to Chiang Mai was pleasant. There was a bathroom at the back of the bus and the scenery was beautiful. I arrived at the Riverside Guest House at 3:00 pm. The three pretty young women who worked the front desk smiled when I arrived and made a graceful *wai*. After eight days on the road, this felt a bit like a homecoming.

I had a bowl of green curry and rice at the mom and pop open air restaurant in the parking lot a block and a half from the guest house, grabbed a waffle filled with coconut on the way home and was in bed by 9:30. I thought I was just tired from travelling. When I woke up at 9:00 the next morning, I knew I was sick.

When the young women who cleaned the rooms knocked on my door at 9:00 am, I said as loudly as I could, "*Mai sabai* (I'm sick)."

"*Mai sabai*," I heard them saying to each other. The small exchange made me feel better, because I was able to communicate in Thai one more time and because the six young women were very cute. When I would waddle out of my room to breakfast at the guesthouse, they would interrupt their work to give me a *wai*, a smile and a "good morning" in English.

Saying they were cute is not a remarkable comment, as I've said before, since almost everyone I've talked to on the subject of Thai

The staff at the Riverside Guesthouse in Chiang Mai

women agrees that the ladies in the Land of Smiles are on the whole some of the most beautiful in the world. They move their slender, almost school girl like bodies with a grace that *farang* (westerners) can't seem to match. The way their black hair falls on their tan shoulders is exquisite. And their smiles! Their radiant smiles make me weak in the knees.

At first I entertained fantasies that the three women at the front desk and the young ladies who did the cleaning liked me better than the other guests, because they always greeted me with such charm. But during the course of the almost four weeks that I stayed at the Riverside, I noticed to my disappointment that they responded that way to everyone.

Cynics might say that the smiles were there to please customers, but based on my observations, Thais are for the most part a genuinely happy people. Eric Weiner in *The Geography of Bliss* ranked the Thais near the top of the list of the happiest people on earth. The smiles are authentic.

A melancholy, brooding temperament like mine doesn't "get" the happiness I see all around me. I like it, but I don't get it. Weiner attributes this abundance of bliss to not thinking too much. "Thais do not buy self-help books or go to therapists or talk endlessly about their problems," he writes. "The Thais, I suspect, are too busy being happy to think about happiness."

The genuine smiles make these beautiful women even more attractive to me, but there's something else which allows me to enjoy their beauty. The many attractive Thai women I've encountered don't seem to know that they are beautiful. Unlike many Americans, both male and female, who seem to be always checking themselves out in the mirror, Thai women seem to be not hung up on themselves.

Karen Connelly was an exchange student in Thailand for a year. In *Dream of a Thousand Lives* (Alternatively entitled *Touch the Dragon*) she was describing seventeen and eighteen year olds when she wrote in her journal,

> These girls are too young, too innocent to be sexy—
> the very word is too vulgar for them—but they
> are living paintings of Oriental beauty and sensuality,
> even in their blue and white school uniforms. I've
> never before seen the grace of beauty that does not
> see itself. Here it is everywhere. (p. 100)

In Thailand this grace of beauty really is everywhere. Connelly was talking about high school girls, but I've seen this grace in women in their twenties, thirties and forties. I've also seen in it children.

Hmong women on Doi Inthanon

I can be a with a group of young women dressed in very short skirts—which they can look good in because of their slim figures—and not feel any sexual vibrations being given off. For me, this is a great relief-- in contrast to the western tendency to sexualize almost everything--because it allows me to enjoy the beauty of these young women in an easy, uncomplicated way.

What I have just said, of course, seems to stand in contradiction to the fact that, by all estimates I've ever read, there are more prostitutes in Thailand than monks. . . . .and there a lot of monks. Connelly says it is due to a double standard in Thai society. In another part of her memoir she wrote,

> My [male] guardians forbid me to be alone with
> Thai men, almost fall over if they see me wearing
> a pair of walking shorts, yet their houses are adorned
> with pictures of naked beauty queens and their weekends
> in Bangkok are full of frolicking in massage parlours.
> (p. 92-93)

One commentator I read on the web said that if a man is a virgin when he gets married he is ridiculed by his friends, while a woman who has had sex is damaged goods.

Dr. Niels Mulder is an anthropologist who has observed Thai society for over thirty years. He has this to say about the smiles on the faces of Thai women who function daily as "the hind legs of the elephant," as the Thai saying goes:

Most Thai women are quite pragmatic about all this.
Where many men often appear to be wish-washy,
spoiled, cocky, and carried away by the greatness
of their schemes, the women are generally hard-working,
responsible and conscientious. . . .In the male
dominated world of Thailand, a smile may mean
anything. . .and behind smiling female grace and
elegance, one often finds powerful, go-getting women.
Nevertheless, even given all that, the Thais appreciate
grace and elegance; things should be beautiful to be
in order, yet this order also requires hard work and
dependability. Which is why it is women who are at
the heart of Thai life. (*Inside Thai Society*, pp. 72-73)

27

Heartwood of the Bodhi Tree

Even though I slept twelve hours both Monday and Tuesday nights, I still felt sick on Wednesday, so I started taking the antibiotics my family doctor back home had prescribed for me to take along.

I had learned from experience. Travelling is hard on my body. The previous year I had gotten sick with flu-like symptoms on my last day in Thailand. That trip had been only two weeks long, so I had decided that I would come prepared for two months away from home in a land where all sorts of different bugs might be entering my system by asking my family doctor back home for a prescription of anti-biotics which I began taking. Within a couple of hours I began feeling better—not great but better.

I felt good enough to drag myself a block down *Thanon Lamphun*, which ran alongside the Mae Ping River, to the Motto coffee ship where a *Nong Bua Sam* member, whose nickname was Fon, was a manager. The antibiotics plus the caffeine in an iced coffee woke me up enough to sit out on their porch and finish the book Bikkhu Buddha Dhatu had given me in the train station in Bangkok.

Much of the book, as it turned out, was critical of many monks whom my *bikkhu* (monk) friend charged with being lax and not adhering strictly to the 227 rules which members of *sangha* (monastic community) promise to keep when ordained. His critique was interesting, but it didn't answer many of the questions I had about Buddhism in general and meditation in particular.

135

So, with my energy coming back, the next day I flagged down a *tuk tuk* which took me to the Suriwong Book Center where I scanned the English book section for answers to my questions. What I was looking for, I thought, was a book on the different kinds of Buddhist meditation—sitting, standing, walking—but I couldn't find any that looked good.

Now, it might sound strange for a Christian to say that the Holy Spirit helped me pick out the book I did. I'm not sure what attracted me to it, the title maybe or the face of the monk on the cover, but the book I picked out from the twenty or so English titles on the shelves was *Heartwood of the Bodhi Tree, the Buddha's Teaching on Voidness* by Buddhadasa Bhikkhu.

I say that the choice was inspired, because when I would tell Thai Buddhists that I was reading Buddhadasa, they universally approved of my choice and all agreed that he was one of the most respected, controversial and influential Thai monks in the Twentieth Century. I also felt kind of led to the book, because even though it said almost nothing about meditation, it confronted me with a Buddhist concept with which I needed to wrestle—*voidness* or *emptiness*.

Not knowing for sure what I had in my hand at that moment, I climbed down the stairs from the book center to street level, bought an iced coffee from the Wawee Coffee Shop next door, sat at a table under a tree on the sidewalk and started to read what the famous *bhikkhu* had to say.

Already in the foreword to the English edition, which was written by a *farang*, I knew I had something important in my hands. Whereas my monk friend in the Bangkok train station, Bikkhu Buddha Dhatu, focused on reforming the practice of Buddhism, Buddhadasa Bhikku's goal was to cut through all of the cultural accretions which had collected over 2556 years and get back to the core of the Buddha's teaching—*sunnata* (*sun atta*, i.e. void of self).

In the preface the translator, Santikaro Bhikkhu, described the context for Buddhadasa's attempt to return to pure teaching or *dhamma*,

For the masses, moral teachings based on
ancient—and not particularly Buddhist—beliefs
about *karma*, rebirth, merit, heaven, and hell
were considered appropriate and sufficient.
Thus, the most profound teachings of the Buddha
were left out of public discourse. . . .The Dhamma
of this word had been lost. (pp. xvi-xvii)

Already on page four, I could see why Buddhadasa was
criticized by many "mainline Buddhists" as an iconoclast. I read,

To call something "a fundamental principle of Buddhism"
is only correct if, first, it is a principle that aims at the
quenching of *dukkha* (pain, misery, suffering) and,
second, it has a logic that one can see for oneself
without having to believe others. (p. 4)

"Therefore," he declared, "the whole question of rebirth [i.e.
reincarnation] is quite foolish and has nothing to do with Buddhism
at all."

"The Buddhist teachings aim to inform us," he continued,
"that there is no person who is a self or belongs to a self."

And just to make sure that this *farang*, whose dictionary at
home (Random House College Dictionary) has 134 words listed with
self as a prefix, got the point, the bhikkhu stated, "The sense of self
is only the false understanding of the ignorant mind. . . .The matter
of 'I' and 'mine," ego and selfishness is the single essential issue of
Buddhism." (p. 5)

I was beginning to understand—I should have realized that
whenever I think I understand something in Thailand I'm at the door
of trouble--that the core of Buddhist teaching was *sunnata*. And,
I thought to my self—pun intended—that this is again looking at
"reality" through a lens with which I'm not familiar.

For the last month I had been having internal debates with

Bikkhu Buddha Dhatu about his assertion that all religions are the same. I only had to read through page fourteen to discover that Buddhadasa seemed to be on my side of this particular issue. He wrote, "The difference between other creeds and Buddhism is that when they eradicated those feelings [self-centeredness, greed, hatred, delusion], they called what remained the 'True Self,' the 'Pure Atman,' the 'Person.'" (pp. 13-14)

"I knew it," I said to myself somewhat triumphantly. "All those pluralist types back home along with my monk friend in the train station are simply projecting their tolerant, simplistic world view on a reality that is complicated, diverse and often inscrutable."

I had been wrestling with Bhikkhu Buddha Dhatu the whole trip, and now I had one of the most respected monks in Thailand as kind of tag team member to help me pin my opponent to the theological floor.

That is until, a few days later, I was reading a talk given by Buddhadasa in 1986 in which he declared, "I would have you understand the heart of Christianity and Buddhism: they say the same thing even though they have been interpreted differently."(*Happiness and Hunger*, 1986)

"Wait a minute," my mind protested. "Didn't you just say a few days ago that Buddhism and other religions are different?" So much for having things figured out. I was looking for easy answers, and this new monk in my life wasn't giving them to me. Now, I had a new person to wrestle with, and he was Olympic class.

I was reminded that spiritually, I was in a foreign country in which, for a Westerner, disorientation is the norm. I had known what to do with the suffering caused by whatever bug it was which was attacking my body. I fought it with antibiotics, sleep and caffeine—a very Western, scientific response—and was winning.

But when it came to figuring Buddhadasa out, I was once again in the deep end of the pool struggling to just keep my head above water.

28

A Gift For Kampan and M

I woke up on Saturday morning knowing that I needed to buy a gift for Kampan and M. They had been gracious hosts when I had arrived in Chiang Mai a month earlier. I wanted to say thank you to them for letting me sleep in their home for five days and knew that they would never accept money.

Giving gifts is a very Thai thing to do. Perhaps more than alcohol in the U.S., feeding people and giving them gifts is the social lubricant in the Land of Smiles. I called Nicky and asked her what would be an appropriate gift. She said flowers or a fruit basket would be nice, and then she added that Kampan would also appreciate me praying for her.

Nicky's suggestion made sense to the small part of my brain that had some understanding of Thai culture. I had been working with the Thai congregation back home for 18 years and had been to Thailand seven times now and was no longer embarrassed by the number of gifts showered on me.

During that time I had been given eight Thai dress shirts--one of them hand made out of silk by a tailor in Chiang Mai—and six polo shirts. I had been taken out to dinner at fancy restaurants. One, The Gallery on the banks of the Mae Ping in Chiang Mai, boasted that Hillary Clinton had dined there. My condo was decorated with wood carvings, vases, a statue and a royal flag, all of which had been given to me as presents. Two years after I began working with the Thai

139

congregation, they gave me an all expenses paid 17 day educational trip to Thailand with a three day stop in Tokyo.

At one point I had said to Pongsak, the pastor of the Thai congregation in Forest Park, "I never give you and Monta presents, but you keep giving them to me."

His face took on a serious look as he replied, "I know, I know, and I don't expect anything from you. It's not part of your culture, except on special occasions like Christmas or birthdays. But, I'm a Thai, and I just wouldn't feel right if I didn't give you gifts and take you out to eat."

What Pastor Pongsak touched on had been one of the major themes in my nearly two decade long relationship with the Thai congregation. When I was with them or in Thailand, I was constantly bumping up against behaviors and attitudes which, frankly, sometimes irritated me or made me feel uncomfortable.

One source of discomfort for me was that Thais tended to look outward for personal orientation in life, while Westerners are conditioned to look inward. Detective Sonchai in *Bangkok Eight* put it this way as he tried to explain how Thai culture worked to his temporary American partner: "There are cultures of guilt and cultures of shame. Yours is a culture of guilt, mine is one of shame."(p. 246)

One example of this outward orientation is the Thai obsession with *face*. Anthropologist Niels Mulder wrote, "The Thai person is highly involved with his presentation. . .as a means of achieving acceptance and status. . . .Often, it appears that outward acceptance spells inner security, and that the distance between one's accepted presentation ('face') and one's emotional self is small."

This looking to others for validation and identity results in a cultural characteristic called *krengchai* which, according to Mulder, is an "awareness and anticipation of the feelings of others." "Krengchai behaviour manifests itself in kindness, self-restraint, tolerance, and the avoidance of interpersonal irritation." Many people I've talked to attribute *krengchai* to the rural roots of Thai culture where maintaining a harmonious social atmosphere is paramount.

When I first became involved with the Thai congregation and then made my first trip to Thailand, I felt like I had died and gone to heaven. Here I was surrounded by people catering to me and trying to anticipate my every need. The more I was with them, however, the more I became frustrated by the lack of intimacy in our relationships. Conversations never got to the level of "how do I feel about that." I didn't feel like I "really knew them."

The irony of my frustration is that I had been raised in a German-American culture in Wisconsin in which self-control was one of the highest virtues, and I had invested many years and thousands of dollars on psycho-therapy in an attempt to get in touch with my inner SELF and learn how to express my feelings. A joke I often told to explain what growing up was like for me goes: "Did you hear about the German who loved his wife so much that once he almost told her?"

Buying a gift for Kampan and M was one of those Thai customs which I didn't find irritating. In this case, my instincts and Thai culture sang in harmony.

As I made my way through the tropical courtyard from my room to the breakfast area, I decided that I would walk to the Rimping Market later in the day. It was only a block away, and I could do my shopping for Kampan on the way home from dinner at my favorite mom and pop restaurant.

As I enjoyed my breakfast of fresh papaya, pineapple and those sweet four inch long bananas, I struck up a conversation with the couple at the table next to me. Turns out they had been living in Beijing for seven years and had come to Chiang Mai for some R & R and continuing education. When I admitted to still feeling like a learner in Thai culture after so many years, they laughed and said that even after seven years of living in China, they felt the same way.

I had heard those same words from many people during my travels, but I needed to hear them again. It's like I had them in my head but couldn't get them into my gut. Hearing someone who shared my experience of reality somehow freed me to feel OK about being a permanent learner in a foreign culture.

My conversation with those ex pats at breakfast made me recall what Dr. Ian Corness had written about living and working as a *farang* in Thailand. As he talked about his inability to figure out Thai women, he wrote,

> It is back to the "the more you know, the less you
> understand" situation, as is always the case
> with *farangs* attempting to comprehend the convoluted
> Thai culture....As a foreigner living here, you have
> to be prepared to drop your own preconceived ideas.
> Unless you have grown up in the village, speak Thai
> as your first language, and understand the Thai family
> culture, you will never, ever, really know. As my [Thai]
> wife says, "*Farang*, they think too much." (*Farang,
> Thailand through the eyes of an ex-pat,* pp. 229-230)

As I thought about always feeling a little disoriented and slightly off balance in Thai culture, I realized how much I depended on the perspective of Western writers who "knew" Thailand better than I did to help me, if not understand this foreign way of life, to at least find some sense of equilibrium.

Kimberly, the FBI agent with whom Detective Sonchai was working in *Bangkok Eight,* was trying to explain to her Thai colleague how she felt after only a few weeks on his turf when she said, "I guess culture shock is more powerful than anyone realizes....I've never felt that way before, like being in a place with no references." (Burdett, p. 221)

Twenty-four pages later, she articulated how I still feel sometimes even after having been with Thais for eighteen years:

You know, back in my country I'm accustomed to
thinking of myself as a pretty bright person. Then
for a few days over here I wondered if I'd been
deceiving myself, and maybe I was a pretty dumb
person. I got over that when I realized I was just
suffering from culture shock, that everyone is dumb
outside their own frame of references. (p. 245)

I realized that many years ago I had moved out of the "tourist
stage," that almost intoxicating feeling people get when they first
visit Thailand that everything there is exotic, dreamy and beautiful.
The honeymoon had ended for me, and, as with most relationships,
there had been times of disillusionment. Letting go of illusions is a
wonderful antidote to disillusionment. Now, whenever I begin to feel
irritation rising in my spleen, I try to say to myself what Thais often
say to each other, "*Mai pen rai*," i.e. never mind or no problem or no
big deal.

I also realized that Thailand wasn't home. I found myself
thinking more about hamburgers and pizza, watching football on
Sunday afternoons, feeling affection from my kids when I visit them,
talking about feelings in my Thursday evening men's group and being
in a place where, for at least some of the time, I would intuitively
understand what was going on around me.

29

Making Peace With Being a Foreigner

Joy, a member of Nong Bua Sam, and her boyfriend picked me up at the Riverside guest house. I took the two baskets of fruit and packages of cookies I had purchased at the Rimping Market for Kampan the night before and loaded them into her car's trunk, before crawling into the back seat. The route Joy took was by now familiar. I recognized many landmarks.

I was still feeling like I was ready to go back home even though I had almost two more weeks left in my travels alone in Thailand. Maybe that's why I reacted to the first part of my morning at the church with irritation.

For one thing, the service started half an hour later than advertised—nothing unusual for Thais. Then the preacher, as usual, spoke two or three times as long as my Western "get to the point" attention span was used to tolerating. Jiraporn and Nicky periodically tried to fill me on what was being said, but, as they say, a lot was lost in the translation—happens all the time. And then, of course, they asked me to say something. I sighed in relief when the last amen was said.

Following these two hours of being annoyed with Thai culture, my whole attitude was transformed by aspects of their world which I experience as blessings rather than irritations. Sanit directed me to a table under the shade of a thatched roof set aside for those of us who were *ajahns* (educated) or elders. Gracious young women served us a banquet of curries, soup, noodle dishes, a spicy salad, omelets and fresh fruit.

The Western part of me isn't used to being treated like a king. Besides, I had never done anything for them, really. All I had done during the last sixteen years was to show up at their doorstep and enjoy their generous hospitality. But that's one of the things about Thai culture that always amazes me. I didn't have to perform. I simply belonged. Part of it was the fact that I was educated and part of it was their respect for my gray hair, but mostly it was because the decision had been made at some point along the way that even though I was not Thai, I had a place at their table.

Back home, when my disorder progressed to a certain point, I was expected to step down as pastor of my congregation and be replaced by someone who could perform according to expectations. In contrast, the Thai congregation, which had been worshiping in our building for fourteen years at that point, started giving me a gift of money every month, because I was their "uncle," and eventually they put me in their preaching rotation even though my speech is slurred.

Likewise, at Nong Bua Sam, Supraporn can only speak in a whisper because of throat surgery done years before, but every Sunday they seated her up front by the altar and have her do something which doesn't tax her voice like saying a prayer. They honor her simply because she has been and always will be their pastor. They will find other people to perform as preachers and teachers, but she will be their pastor as long as she lives. Her place and my place at Nong Bua Sam are not based on performance but on our relationship to the community.

After lunch, a young woman I knew named An asked if I had ever thought about living in Thailand. My enjoyment of their gracious hospitality, I guess, had been obvious. Besides, I kept coming back. I only hesitated for a moment, though, before saying, "No. I love coming here, but this isn't home."

Nicky brought Kampan and M over to where I was sitting, so I could give my thank you gifts to them. I don't think Kampan understood all of my prayer which, as requested, accompanied the gifts, but that didn't seem to matter to her. Apparently, she didn't need to understand everything for the act to be meaningful.

145

Aware that I would be leaving Chiang Mai in four days, we began saying our goodbyes. All of the young women in the congregation gathered around me for a photo op and giggled when I told them that they made me feel young. Fae and An offered to drive me back to the Riverside, and, while I crawled into the car, the older women lined up along the driveway. As we passed them on the way out they waved, and, on cue from Jiraporn, they all sang out, "We love you."

Surrounded by beauty at Nong Bua Sam Church

* * *

I asked Fae and An to drop me off at the Anusan Market which is part of Chiang Mai's night bazaar. I waddled over to Mohr Moo, my favorite open air restaurant at Anusan, and ordered pad Thai and a Singha beer. I bought some thank you treats for the women at the Riverside who had treated me with such kindness and ended the evening with a foot massage.

Having one of those tiny Thai women with strong hands work on my feet and lower legs for an hour as I reclined in one of their comfortable chairs is, in my experience, not only relaxing but also healing and calming. That evening it also provided a spiritual space in which I could digest the emotions and experiences of the last few days.

Foot massage at Anusan Market

What struck me first is that a lot of religion back home is like a foot massage, i.e. it's intended to heal and comfort people who are shopping around in the spiritual marketplace for something which can make them feel more peaceful and balanced in a changing, turbulent world. You might call it *therapeutic religion.* In fact, I've had several American Buddhists tell me to take what I need from them and leave the rest alone.

That made me recall how I had responded to An when she asked if I had ever thought about living in Thailand. In saying that Thailand wasn't home, I decided that what I meant was that living here would be too much work. Subconsciously, I had done a cultural cost/benefit analysis and had concluded that the many benefits weren't worth the cost. Coming to Thailand once a year for two weeks was an exciting adventure, but for the long haul I preferred the familiar comforts of home

What happened then startled me. My mind freely associated with the Gospel of Matthew which I had been reading during my daily morning prayer time. Again and again, Matthew tells about the disciples getting thrown off balance and disoriented by Jesus' statements: eg. *the last shall be first* or *love your enemies* or *if you want to live, you have to die* or *those who love father and mother more than me are not worthy of the kingdom of God.*

Jesus kept talking about the kingdom of God as if it were a foreign country where life would be better than, in what those twelve guys thought of as, their home. It might be better, but to those disciples it sure wasn't comfortable. Half the time they didn't understand what the Teacher was saying, so he'd paraphrase the concepts into parables which they often didn't get either. They couldn't pick up on the cultural cues in this new kingdom. They spoke with an accent, as it were. They felt disoriented, like they were always in the position of children who needed to be shown how to proceed. Somehow being with Jesus made them feel secure. Apart from him they were out of their element.

Every time I've come to Thailand I've had to go through the process of letting go of the feeling that I know what I'm doing and one more time find a tolerable degree of comfort in always being a learner. I have to find a way to accept that I'll always be a *farang* in a foreign land, always need a guide to tell me where I am and show me where to go. After being in Thailand for six weeks, I had had enough of adventure and wanted to go back to where I felt like I knew my way around.

Feeling in control, apparently, is a big issue for us humans. The previous year I had been camping in Northern Wisconsin for three days at the beginning of October. At night, the temperature would plunge to below freezing, so after sundown I would build a fire to keep warm until bedtime. When I couldn't fight off sleep anymore, I'd hustle into my tent and quickly crawl into my sleeping bag without taking off my jeans and sweater.

Each morning I would notice that there would be frost on the ground as I made my way from the warmth of my sleeping bag to the car where I would immediately start the engine and turn the on heater, so I wouldn't die of hypothermia while changing into clean clothes. But by noon, the sun would have heated the land to almost seventy degrees, the extravagant colors of the changing leaves would be reflected in clear blue lakes, and I would luxuriate in the powerful silence of the north woods.

During the afternoon of my second day, I noticed a camper as big as a bus roll into the campground. The folks in that camper had a lot more control regarding their comfort than I did. They weren't anywhere near as exposed to the elements as I was, yet I felt a little sorry for them. They were keeping nature at a distance, as it were. They were avoiding the discomforts of sleeping in a tent, but I couldn't help believing that they weren't appreciating the warmth of the noonday sun on the back of their neck as much either.

If it's true that the world is shrinking, it seems to me that we have a choice. In regard to other cultures, we can hole up in our camper and only step outside when the conditions are the way we like them or we can sleep in a tent and be more vulnerable to the elements. On the one hand, I wouldn't want to sleep in a tent every night. On the other hand, I'm pretty sure that being obsessed with comfort and control leads to missing out on much of that unpredictable, mysterious, turbulent experience called life.

I'm sure my two hour friend, whom I had met in Lampang and who had fumbled around Asia by himself for a year, would understand what I was thinking. I wasn't sure what the Buddha would say about all of this, but that question would have to wait. My foot massage was over. I flagged down a *tuk tuk*, was in my room in fifteen minutes, flopped in bed and slept like a rock.

30

Missionaries

As I've said before, I'm never sure of myself in Thai culture. When I look at a menu, I'm not certain if the food listed is *peht mak* (very spicy hot) or *mai peht* (not spicy). I'm never sure when I should take my shoes off before entering a building or when it's OK to leave them on. I still have not learned all the rules about when I should initiate a *wai* and when I should wait for the other person to begin the greeting. Because I always feel like a disoriented *farang*, I covet opportunities to talk with people who know their way around better than I do to help get some sense of orientation.

That's why I like to talk to missionaries, the ones who have been in Thailand a long time. They don't always have the answers, but at least they say they don't in words I understand!

Bruce Rowe tanslating for me at Nong Bua Sam Church

I've known Bruce and Lori Rowe since 1994 when I visited Chiang Mai for the first time. They came to Thailand as independently funded missionaries in 1992. Bruce is a computer guy who has devoted all his time to supporting churches with their communication and networking needs. Lori is a nurse who got involved with HIV/AIDS work with the tribal people living in the hills around Chiang Mai They picked me up at the guesthouse, and we had lunch together at a noodle shop. The conversation shifted at one point to the topic of missionaries. Years ago, Bruce said, the missionary strategy was based on a model of conversion that tried to show that Buddhism is wrong and that Christianity has the truth.

They don't do that anymore, he continued, partly because most missionaries are now in back up roles like the work he does with computers. It's almost universally accepted among Western church workers that Thais communicate better with their neighbors than *farang* do. But more importantly, most missionaries accept that the rational, argumentative approach not only did not work—after over 150 years of missionary activity, Thailand is only 1% Christian—but it also is really contrary to the gospel which they are trying to preach.

Bruce said that the Thai Christians he works with don't talk about Buddhism—negatively or positively—hardly at all. Partly it's because Thais are becoming less and less religious, i.e. Buddhism for many is no longer the organizing force in their psyche that it used to be. But, more importantly, Thai Christians have learned that they don't have to put down Buddha in order to share their love of Jesus. It's about relationships more than ideas, although ideas—i.e. doctrine--still matter.

Bruce's comments made me remember a conversation I had two years ago with four Thais in their twenties who had recently been baptized and were studying at a Bible school in Bangkok. When asked why they became Christian, they all said that in this religion they felt loved. They didn't even mention doctrine or metaphysics.

When I talk about Thailand to my friends back home, some of the more liberal ones say that they are against sending missionaries anywhere, that missionaries embody that whole colonial, imperialistic, superior attitude which they disdain. They have heard stories about missionary arrogance and cultural insensitivity, some of which are true, of course.

It was the picture of exclusivist "we're right and you're wrong" missionaries that my liberal friends had in their minds. Buddhadasa, though highly motivated to dialog with Christians, also had the negative images of missionaries in his mind when he said, "Those missionaries who claim Dhamma as their own are oppressors, propagating their own Dhamma as different and better, as the only true Dhamma."

As I listened to Bruce and Lori tell stories about their work in Chiang Mai, however, I got to thinking. First, I've never met an arrogant, insensitive missionary in my travels to Thailand. I'm sure there are some, but I haven't met them. Like Prince Damrong said in 1928, the Christian missionaries have done a lot of good in Thailand.

Second, I've met several Buddhist "missionaries" to the U.S. None of them—and they've all been American--have been arrogant either. In fact, most work hard at adapting their teaching to what Americans can relate to. In terms of their motivation, it's really quite simple. They've encountered a belief system which they feel has changed their lives, and they can't wait to share what they've experienced with others. The same is true, as far as I can tell, for the Christian missionaries I've met in the Land of Smiles.

The conversation then segued onto the subject of church politics. Bruce and Lorie told me that a lot of the ordinary church members they talk to were discouraged by what happened in the election that had recently taken place in the Church of Christ in Thailand, the denomination with which I'm most familiar. From the perspective of the person in the pew, the election was more about power and privilege than about servant leadership. And, these were Thai Christians talking about their own Thai leaders.

It occurred to me that Bruce and Lori were identifying more with the ordinary guy in the pew than with those who had power in the church. They had invested most of their adult lives in Thailand and had raised their three sons there. They would be the first to acknowledge that they are flawed human beings, but they had adapted themselves to Thailand rather than trying to reshape Thailand in their image. They still thought of the U.S. as home, but they had developed a very realistic and affectionate appreciation for this Asian land in which they are long term sojourners.

*   *   *

After lunch, the Rowes dropped me off at the McGilvery College of Divinity, a Church of Christ in Thailand seminary which is part of Payap Universtity. There I would have a chance to gain a little more insight into Thai culture from two more people I respected.

Satanun Boonyakiat is the dean of the seminary and Karsten van Staveren is the school's international program director. Without knowing what Bruce and Lori had talked about, they soon began venting their feelings and stating thoughts about leadership in the Thai church.

"This expectation that you treat everyone as a threat to your power once you rise to the top," Karsten said, "that is something that has to change."

Satanun agreed and blamed the Western missionaries, not for the way they exercised power when they had it, but for the way they handed power over to the Thais. "I think missionaries have done wonderful ministries in Thailand in the past and have started many innovative ministries here," he explained, "but I don't think they did enough to help the Thai leaders take over. Missionaries and Thai leaders didn't really have a chance to work together, to create an atmosphere in which they can work together to help the younger Thai generation become ready for the job."

"This sounds so familiar," I thought as I listened. "It's the same issue being debated back home regarding how the U.S. should leave Iraq and Afghanistan."

Karsten added that the extreme respect for elders in Thai culture sometimes gets in the way of effective leadership. "In the Netherlands [where he earned his M.Div. degree]," he said, "when you are 35 you are over the hill. In Thailand, starting at 35 maybe you get a little responsibility; a little more when you pass 50 and you really get responsibility when you are over 60 or 65. By doing things that way you throw away a lot of potential that is there."

Both men are in their thirties. "We are sitting here with Ajahn Satanun," he continued. "In a sense it is a miracle [that he is dean] because according to Thai culture there should be someone much older. His appointment was born out of need. There was no one else qualified to do this job."

He added that the younger generation in the church is getting fed up to the point where they don't want to continue this way, but that the solution is not to copy a model from the West which doesn't fit Thai culture. "Leading by example," he concluded, "is much more what changes churches, which makes people understand. You lead by the example of your life more than by writing plans."

Again I got to thinking, "This sounds very much like the disillusionment many Americans feel about politicians. In my own state of Illinois, Rod Blagojevich, a former governor, would be convicted on 17 counts a few months later.

The two *ajahns* also mentioned the need for students to learn how to analyze their own culture, so that in their preaching they would be better able to show how the Christian faith addresses the questions people in Thai society are asking, i.e. to make religion relevant. They said that one way to do this is to enable more students to study abroad.

This puzzled me. "How can studying in the U.S., Australia or Europe help Thais better understand their own culture?" I asked.

Satanun replied that it is a matter of gaining perspective. He earned his Ph.D. at Fuller Seminary in California. It's not about imposing models that work in the American context on the Thai church, he explained, but of attaining a place where you can observe your own culture more objectively.

Karsten was raised in Thailand by Dutch parents, studied at a university (Utrecht) in the Netherlands and is now teaching back in Thailand. "I'm a person in between cultures," he said, "which means that I have enough distance to reflect on Thai culture, but I'm close enough to also love it. Understanding your own culture is one of the most difficult things if you have never been outside of it."

I left McGilvery not so much with a greater understanding of Thailand but with a better handle on why I had needed to spend 40 days alone in Thailand. If you compare making sense out of life to putting together a 1000 piece puzzle, until you have been thrown into another culture deeply enough to get thoroughly disoriented, it's like trying to put the puzzle pieces together by referring to the picture printed on the wrong box cover.

You think you know, you imagine what the pieces should look like when you've assembled them completely but get frustrated when they don't fit together in a way that produces the picture you want. It's not until you get an accurate picture that you start to fit the pieces together.

Buddhadasa in a 1969 essay called *No Religion* talked about how the lenses you are looking through determine what you see: "We stumble on past the things that we should receive, that would benefit us, because our own views are a prison that confines us. . . ."(pp. 185-186).

A few days later I picked up a book by the Venerable Acariya Thoon Khippapanyo entitled *Change Your View, Change Your Life* in which he argued for pretty much the same thing. He wrote, "Buddhism emerged in the world because of Prince Siddhattha's paradigm shift."(p. 2)

He added, "A change in perception requires insight-wisdom, as one discerns which mindsets are incorrect, and which are correct. Discernment through reason that is based on the undisputable truth will produce a righteous paradigm."(p. 4)

When I left home at the beginning of December on United Airlines flight #881, I imagined that my time alone in Thailand would be a wilderness experience like Jesus had for forty days or Moses and the people of Israel went through for forty years. It would be full of struggles with demons which I had avoided facing until now, a test of my character.

I have to admit that I was at this point a little disappointed that there had been no epic battles like the one that the four children fought with Aslan in Narnia against the wicked witch. I had been given no chance to emerge from the forty days a spiritual hero. Instead, all that I had experienced was the frequent feeling, like those four children, of not knowing what I was doing in a very foreign land, of having lenses in my intellectual glasses which prevented me from understanding the Thai worldview. Maybe that's what was going on—a little deconstruction to prepare the way for some mental/spiritual reconstruction.

I caught a *tuk tuk* and was home at the Riverside in ten minutes. "I need a drink," I thought, feeling overwhelmed by all the input my brain had received that day, so I waddled down to a coffee shop next to the Rimping Market and ordered a big iced coffee.

What would the Buddha say about all of this?
What would Jesus say?

I sat down in the terrace outside Rimping, sipped my iced coffee and started writing in my journal. A few of the pieces seemed to be fitting together for the first time.

31

Spirit Houses

I was writing as fast as I could in my journal as a way of processing the conversations I had with Bruce and Lori during lunch and with Satanun and Karsten at the seminary. Every few minutes, I'd look up, take a sip of iced coffee, watch the traffic on *Thanon Chiang Mai Lamphun* and gather myself up for the next burst of writing.

During those short breaks, I noticed several people pausing in front of the big *san phra poom* (spirit house) outside the coffee shop, making a *wai* and a small bow, and then continuing on their way. One in maybe every three people passing by would do this, and every once in awhile, one of them would linger with a prolonged *wai*, hands together and head bowed, as if they were praying.

Almost everyone in Thailand has one or two spirit houses standing in a corner of their property, inside their home or standing outside their business. In every town, you'll see dealers with spirit houses of all colors and sizes standing in rows like cars in an auto dealership parking lot in the States.

When I first came to Thailand, watching people praying in front of a spirit house or in a *wat* would confuse me. In college I had taken a course on world religions in which I learned the four noble truths: 1) All life is sorrow and suffering; 2) suffering stems from craving; 3) the end of suffering is achieved by the end of craving; 4) the way to end craving is by following the Eightfold Path of right view, right intention, right speech, right action, right livelihood, right effort, right mindfulness and right concentration.

Spirit house

In Buddhism, I had learned, achieving enlightenment and *nirvana* is all up to the individual. Gods, if there are any, are irrelevant. Praying for help instead of detaching from desire is just a sign that you still don't get it.

So I walk into *Wat Phra Kaew* in 1994—which is sort of like the national "cathedral," if you will, for Thai Buddhists—and I see people kneeling and offering hard boiled eggs, lotus blossoms and incense sticks. It was another of those "the more you see, the less you know" kind of moments.

Praying at a wat   *Spririt House with devotional offerings*

As usual I went to English speaking observers of Thai culture to help me sort out the puzzles pieces which weren't fitting together the way I thought they should. I talked to Thais I knew and all of them told me more or less what Donald Swearer has written in *The Buddhist World of Southeast Asia*: "All too often a textbook picture of Theravada Buddhism bears little resemblance to the actual practice of

Buddhism in Southeast Asia." (p. 1)

I learned that Buddhism as practiced by your average person in Thailand is a syncretistic blending of Buddhism and animism. . .and probably astrology and a dash of Hinduism. That's where the spirit houses fit in. Contrary to what I read in my college textbook, traditional Thais live in a world full of spirits and powers.

The spirits, it appears to me, are like neighbors. If you treat them right, they won't bother you, and maybe they'll even help you out in a time of need. But neglect them, and you might pay a price. So, every day or two you need to make an offering to the spirit of your place. I've seen everything from the standard incense sticks to orange soda to coconuts to money to cans of beer to bowls of rice placed in front of spirit houses.

I heard that you have to get to know the particular personality of the spirit of your property in order to know what will keep it happy. I even heard that one guy figured out that the spirit of his land liked pornography, so from time to time he'd place a Playboy magazine next to its house.

Somehow the marriage of a non-theistic religion like Buddhism and the animistic world view filled with spirits and powers everywhere has functioned fairly well in the Thai cultural ecology for centuries. Buddhist meditation works for the forces you can't control, but believing you can influence powers greater than you through prayer and offerings can make you feel you have some control of what you will encounter on a day to day basis.

Swearer puts it this way: "To be sure, the Theravada Buddhism of Southeast Asia, not unlike other great historic religions, defines ideal goals of moral perfection and ultimate self-transformation, and the means to attain them, but at the same time. . .provides the means by which people cope with day-to-day problems of life as well as a rationale to justify worldly pursuits."(p. 2)

And, of course, that's pretty much the way it is back home. Most of my friends can recite what they were taught in religion classes

while growing up, but as adults they have separated out what is doable
by human beings from what is possible only for the Mother Theresas
and Martin Luther Kings among us. They edit what they were taught
enough to allow them to function in the Monday through Friday
world.

They'll drive an hour or two into Indiana to visit an Amish
settlement and think, "Wow, those people really live what they believe!"
Then they return home, tell all their friends what a good experience it
was and go on living the way they had before.

In both the East and the West, Maslow's hierarchy of needs
trumps both the Four Noble Truths and the Sermon on the Mount.
To take all that stuff seriously, the thinking goes, you'd have to become
a monk. The kingdom of God, as it were, doesn't work in the real
world. Neither does the Eightfold Path.

I have to admit that I've always felt a bit of a connection with
animists. I spent a lot of time in nature while growing up and often
felt like there was something about nature--Lake Michigan during a
storm or a friendly chickadee or the stillness I felt when I was alone
in the woods—some "thing" with which I could have a relationship.
When I read that Mohicans would thank the spirit of the deer they
had just killed in order to feed their family, I could kind of relate to
that reverential way of leaning into life.

Maybe that's why, by percentage, tribal people are ten times
more likely to become Christian than ethnic Thais. In fact, I heard
that 40% of all Christians in Thailand are tribal people even though
they comprise only 10% of the population at most. Tribal people are
strictly animists, and as such perhaps they can relate to the belief in
the existence of a spiritual being which humans can communicate
with better than a Buddhist who focuses on detachment through
meditation.

What I couldn't resonate to is this understanding that the
spirits could harm you. I grew up with a romantic picture of Native
American animism in which the spirits in the trees and animals and

streams were all smiling at me kindly as I walked through the woods. In Thailand, the spirits are capable of messing with you and even harming you if you don't keep them happy. That's why, just a few blocks from *Wat Phra Kaew* in Bangkok there is a large amulet market where you can buy all kinds of spiritual "Kevlar vests" to protect you from ornery spirits.

Buddhadasa writes that this is all nonsense which deludes people and distracts them from letting go of all attachments. In fact, the more I learned about him, the more I compared Buddhadasa to my childhood religious hero, Martin Luther.

Luther, like Buddhadasa, had been a monk. He had protested the selling of indulgences as having nothing to do with Jesus' teaching in the Bible. Likewise, the famous Thai Buddhist monk railed against fortune telling, amulets, astrology and animistic spirit houses as having nothing to do with the Buddha's teaching. He urged Buddhists to return to the ancient Pali texts in the same way that Luther exhorted Christians to base their thinking about God on the Bible alone.

A lot of Buddhists in Thailand, especially lay people, would respond to Buddhadasa's critique of their syncretism by saying, "It's easy for you to criticize us, you who sit and meditate all day. You don't have to deal with raising kids, pleasing your spouse and running a business. Believing in spirits and buying amulets helps us deal with the pressures of reality."

It was then that I noticed a slight change in my reflecting. Instead of asking "what would the Buddha say," I asked myself "what would Buddhadasa say?" And I remembered him contending in *Heartwood of the Bodhi Tree* that what most people think is real is merely "foolishness and delusion."(p. 50)

OK, so what would Jesus say? My thoughts shifted to the Sermon on the Mount. See the birds in the air, said Jesus. See the lilies. God takes care of them. So why are you anxious about being able to function in the "real" world. "Seek first the kingdom of God," he taught his followers, "and all these things will—somehow--be yours as well." If I read the text correctly, Jesus is saying that the Kingdom of God is more "real" than the "real world."

I shouldn't have looked up from my writing frenzy, I realized. Instead of finding some order in the scattered puzzle pieces in front of me, watching people pray at the spirit house added even more pieces to my confusion.

32

BILL YODER

One man with whom I always try to get together when I'm in Chiang Mai is a missionary named Bill Yoder. Bill came to Chiang Mai in 1963, when I was a sophomore in high school, and has been in Thailand pretty much ever since. When he retired a couple years ago, he was the Dean of the McGilvery College of Divinity, the post which Satanun now holds.

Bill has invested the last 48 years of his life in the Thai people in general and in the Christian church in Thailand in particular. Single his whole life, he was the foster parent for 27 Thai children, having up to seven of them in his home at one time. My friend Sanit at the Nong Bua Sam Church is one of Bill's "children." Bill has a plot purchased in the missionary cemetery in Chiang Mai, a pretty clear indication that for him Thailand is home.

Bill Yoder surrounded by choir

Thailand is his home now, yet he steadfastly maintains that he will never be Thai. A few years ago he acknowledged, with a sheepish smile, that when he first arrived in Chiang Mai he had fantasies of becoming Thai. Although he speaks, what my Thai pastor back home calls perfect Thai, he told me that he learned early on that he would always be an American.

From what I have gathered, the Thais he teaches and works with don't want him to become a Thai. They appreciate how hard he has worked at adapting to their culture, but they also appreciate the perspective he brings to them precisely because he is a *farang*. He is a striking example of what Karsten and Satanun were talking about when they told me they wished more of their students could study abroad—to gain a point view from which they could observe their own culture as if for the first time. "The Thais sometimes say to me," Bill told me a few years ago, "that I understand Thailand better than they do."

When I asked him how he has changed during his almost half century long sojourn in Thailand, he exclaimed, "Oh my gosh! I came here as a naïve graduate of the College of Wooster in Ohio. I'd never been outside the U.S. except for Canada. My whole life has changed dramatically."

His relationship with God in particular was changed by two experiences. One was his contact with Christians living in Thailand who had survived World War II. Some were Chinese who had immigrated to Thailand when Mao came into power in 1949, and some were Thais who had lived through what amounted to but was never officially called a Japanese occupation.

"These were people," he said, "who were much older than I who had lived through a great deal of persecution because they were Christian." He explained that he came to Thailand as a "cultural Christian." He was brought up in the church and thought of America has a Christian nation.

"It was quite startling for me," he continued, "to find people in real life who had consciously made the decision to make their faith the number one thing in their lives and to possibly defend their right to do that even possibly with their lives."

"I suddenly thought 'why is something like belief in Jesus Christ so vitally important to these people when it isn't to me, and I'm supposed to be a Christian.'" He laughed and added, "That started me thinking."

The second experience was his encounter with Buddhism. During his first two years in Chiang Mai he taught English to the novices and some of the monks at *Wat Phra Singh* on Saturday mornings, and after lunch he and the monks would sometimes get into discussions about religion. He said of those discussions,

> It was a turning point in my life to know that
> there were distinct differences between world views,
> and not everybody thinks the same. I also discovered
> that I was probably thinking more like a Christian
> than I thought I was. I didn't find anything wrong
> with what they were teaching, but it wasn't what
> I felt was germane in the situation.

"What distracted me so much with Buddhism," he recalled, "was the idea of detachment." He remembered the abbot of the *wat* using an example in his preaching of a man being attacked by a pack of dogs. The normal human reaction, said the abbot, is to help the man, but it's best to not get involved, because, first, the man must have done something to make the dogs attack him and second, you might get bitten yourself if you intervene.

"I remember sitting on the temple floor," Bill told me, "and wanting to stand up and say, 'No. How can you say that? It is not natural for human being to want to help the person. It's natural for humans to want to protect themselves.' And second, that is just the opposite of what Jesus is asking us to do. Jesus calls us to try to help, even if it means that we get hurt in the process."

"That's an example," he added, "of how I became more of a convinced follower of Christ than I originally ever thought I was. I sometimes say that I was converted to Christianity by the Buddhists."

Yoder's comment made me think of a young woman back home who took advantage of an opportunity at her college to wear an hijab, a Muslim headscarf, for a week. Not only did she become closer to Muslim coeds at her school, but the experience also made her stronger in her Christian faith. "You can only really know your own faith fully," she said, "when you experience other faiths."

Dr. Donald Swearer, who was himself a missionary in Thailand 1957-1960, stated,

> Indeed, it is not overstating the case to say that
> Buddhism has enlarged and deepened my own
> faith. . . My intention in these lectures is to point
> to some of the ways in which Christian thinking
> can be deepened and broadened by Buddhism."
> (quoted in Bantoon Boon-itt, *A Study of the Dialogue
> between Christianity and Theravada Buddhism in Thailand*)

When I asked Yoder what he thinks about Buddhism now, he responded with a comment about Christianity:

> I think that religions are creations of human
> beings. Christianity is a religion, and as a religion it
> has got to be flawed, because it is a human
> construct. When we talk about Jesus Christ,
> however, we're talking about a relationship that
> has become extremely existential and real in
> someone's experience and has little to do with religion.

For me, listening to Bill reflect on his life was like going to a play and hearing an actor speak lines which feel like they were written about me. He had put into words my ambivalence about Buddhism. On the one hand I had always been attracted to the peaceful ambience in small town *wats*, the serene way the monks kind of float through life, the emphasis on the introspective life.

But in the end, like Bill, I just couldn't buy the detachment thing. I saw how it was useful psychologically in not letting critical people get to me, but not as a fundamental way of leaning into life. The most important time of the year for me is what some Christians call the Triduum, ie. Maundy Thursday, Good Friday and Easter. Others call it Jesus' Passion.

For Buddhists, the paradigm seems to be the Buddha sitting under the Bodhi Tree achieving enlightenment. For Christians it is Jesus dying on the cross. For Buddhists the challenge is to **detach** from everything and everyone including your self(sic). For Christians the goal is to **attach** unconditionally to the only One worthy of that kind of trust.

I thought about how Buddhadasa Bhikkhu would react to Bill Yoder and decided that he would reply that everything my missionary friend was saying was delusional, really. If you just look at things objectively, he would say, you would see that passion and attachments only produce suffering.

I remember him writing that you don't have to accept what he's saying on his authority. "The listener can recognize the truth of every word of the answers," he wrote, "without having to believe them blindly and can see their truth more and more clearly until he understands for himself."

I can just see him living in the U.S. for a couple years, dialoging every week with Christians and returning to Thailand more convinced than ever of the truth of *dhamma* (Buddhist teaching). And I couldn't help going back to my working hypothesis that each religion or world view is like a lens through which believers view the phenomena of their lives—I keep coming back to the metaphor of the lens. No one "sees" objectively. Everyone views life through some sort of lens. The result is that we see what we believe. There are no exceptions. The trick is to find the lens which focuses your mind on that which is most important.

And that got me a little depressed, because it seemed to me that there was no way for Buddhists to understand my faith profoundly unless they took off their spiritual glasses and looked at life through my lenses. And, I knew that I was not willing to set my faith aside for the sake of really understanding the *dhamma*.

There are many things which the two religions share, especially regarding ethics. We can learn from each other as well. Buddhism has a lot to teach Christians about the practice of meditating, for example. But increasingly, I was coming to the conclusion that regarding ultimate truth, the two religions were polar opposites.

So, reading Buddhadasa's statement that Christianity and Buddhism were essentially the same continued to be a thorn in my theological flesh. Everyone respected his intellect, but I just couldn't understand how he could declare that Buddhism alone understands that the *self* is an illusion and that detachment was the door to *nibbana* on the one hand and then on the other hand contend that the two religions are the same.

I could try to understand Buddhism intellectually, of course, and to a degree I have a better grasp of it than any of my friends. But trying to understand Buddhism without practicing it, without diving into it with no reservations, is like trying to understand what it's like to be married by reading a book about it while remaining single.

And then I recalled what Bill had said about the difference between Christianity as a human construct and an existential relationship with Jesus. I had gotten pretty good at observing life through the lens of the Christian religion, but I began to wonder if I had any clue of how the way I live my life looks from the point of view of the kingdom of God which Jesus talked about so much. I wondered how my view of "reality" would change if I were so committed to life in God's Kingdom that I'd be willing to die for it.

33

Sanuk

I waited outside the Riverside guesthouse for Nicky and M to pick me up. On Sunday, Sanit had announced that he was hosting a goodbye dinner for me at the Airport Restaurant and that all the twenty somethings in the congregation were invited.

This was fine with me, since most of the young adults at Nong Bua Sam are female and very attractive. What made me feel even better is that the young women got excited about the prospect of a fun outing. A young woman named An went so far as to declare that everyone should wear *si faa* (light blue) clothing to make the outing more fun.

My first reaction was to get excited myself, but on the way home my anticipation got tempered by memories of Thais not doing what they said they would do. It wasn't that they had been malicious or deceitful. It was, I learned, partly due to that Thai mindset I mentioned previously called *kreng jai*.

If you put a negative spin on *kreng jai* you might describe it as not saying what you really think; telling people what you think they want to hear; avoidance of even small conflicts; fear of being an individual.

I've learned that when Thais say something nice to me, they have an honest desire to make me feel good. If you are Thai, you understand how the game works. You understand that if Thai friends say they will take you to the beach at Pattaya on Saturday, they are showing you that they are sensitive to what you would enjoy doing, but that doesn't mean they will actually follow up and do that. Thais understand that an initial expression of interest in doing something is not the same as a firm commitment. To a Westerner, it could feel like being dishonest.

Nicky and M came right on time, and we arrived at the Airport Restaurant on schedule. No one else was there. In fact, we waited for half an hour alone, and I was starving. What's more, mosquitoes were coming out and it was getting uncomfortably cool. Nicky and M were working on Western time. The rest were following Thai time.

Sanit arrived with two of the young women, and two more came later on. That was all. I knew Sanit would be there like he said he would. So would Nicky and M. They are bi-cultural enough to be able to function according to both Western and Eastern values.

In spite of knowing that the big send off party might not materialize as advertised, I still felt some irritation. "Why can't these people do things the right way?" I muttered to myself and then immediately felt guilty for being so insensitive to another culture.

Sanit, as always, was a gracious host and ordered up a banquet of delicious sea food. Many members of Nong Bua Sam refer to him as *pi* (elder). Some even say *Kuhn* (an even more respectful term) before his name when addressing him or talking about him, and he takes his role very seriously. He and Jiraporn have no children and, much like Bill Yoder did with his foster children, they take care of the members of the church as if they were family.

After the meal, the group wanted to have some *sanuk,* another concept I've mentioned before and which is easier for me to understand than *kreng jai*. It means having fun, but more than that it means having fun in almost everything you do. Mulder calls it an antidote to the status consciousness and expectations of proper presentation in Thai society. (p. 65) I have been in many situations where Thais have played the silliest games and have so much fun.

I was with a youth group a few years before at a church in Nakon Protom and they decided to play a game called "bip, bop, bup." We divided into teams of three and when the leader pointed at a team they had to quickly stand and one would say "bip," the next "bop," and the third "bup." Then they would point to another team who would have to do the same. When your team messed up the drill, you were out of the game, but that wasn't a big deal, because you could still have fun laughing at how the other teams would mess up the same way your team did.

The teams were mildly competitive, but the main idea was to laugh at each other and yourself and simply have a playful good time. The Thais are so good at this, and I'm so uncomfortable, even after eighteen years of being with them. I feel so self-conscious, so *anal* as some of my friends would say. I try. I really try to let go of my inhibitions, but to this day I have to work hard at becoming playful.

So the group decided that to have fun, I would go around the table and ask each individual a question. I knew the rules and tried hard to think of questions which would allow these young adults to respond with light hearted, silly answers. But I didn't quite get to where they wanted to be. They were very gracious and laughed dutifully but everyone was just a little bit uncomfortable with the realization that we were dancing to slightly different rhythms.

On the one hand, the discomfort I felt made me want to return to the cultural comforts of home even more. On the other hand, the discomfort was one more reminder of how difficult multicultural living is. People back home proudly boast that their kids' school is multicultural. What they mean is that it is multiracial, which is no mean accomplishment given America's history.

But, those who say their kids' school is multicultural don't seem to realize that the people of color and whose primary language is other than English have probably come 90% of the way across the bridge to facilitate the diversity and we whites have come out our comfort zone only a few steps. Having a day on which the children wear traditional ethnic costumes and bring their favorite food from home does not make the school's culture "multi." It's still a mono-culture as long as the kids who are from different cultures are doing 90% of the adapting.

There at the Airport Restaurant in Chiang Mai, Thailand the Thai people at my table were speaking English so that I could feel part of the group. Even the worst English speaker in my group was far more fluent in my language than I was in theirs.

Over the years I've received a lot of praise for being the pastor of a congregation which was 25% black, 10% Hispanic and 65% white and which had been a partner in ministry for 18 years with the Thai congregation which shared the same building. The reality is that the only thing that I and the white members did was to open the door. After those minority folks got inside, they did most of the hard work.

34

BRIDGING THE CULTURAL CHASM

I woke up that Thursday morning, Jan. 20, 2011, to mixed emotions. There was some sadness at saying good bye to friends in Chiang Mai. There was some feeling of anticipation of getting out of "a culture that doesn't work the way it is supposed to." I was looking forward to going home.

And, on top of all of that, I was a little anxious about getting a ticket for the train. I had been to the train station the day before, but when I asked for a ticket for a sleeper car on the train to Bangkok on the following day, the ticket agent said that the computers were down. I wasn't caught completely off guard by this news, because it had happened to me twice on this trip alone—once at the bank in Lampang and once at the train station on the border with Cambodia.

So, I got up early, ate breakfast for the last time in the Riverside House, checked my emails at the computer in the front office, gave little gifts to each of the staff, collected my bags and hailed a *tuk tuk*. When I arrived at the train station, I went straight to the ticket window and, after taking a deep breath, asked for a ticket for a sleeper car on the 4:00 pm train to Bangkok. To my relief, the agent typed in the appropriate information and out of the printer came my ticket. I paid my 800 baht ($27) and found a chair in the shade where I could sit down.

Suddenly, with the worries about getting a ticket taken care of, my mood changed. What I felt was a kind of aloneness. I knew it wasn't loneliness, because I found myself being OK with sitting without company for the six hours until the train would leave. It was something more basic than not having someone to talk to.

"Oh well," I thought, "maybe I'll figure it out as the day goes along."

As I was taking out my pocket Bible from my backpack to do my morning prayers, I felt my mobile phone vibrating in my pocket.

"Pastor Holmes, this is Nicky. Did you get your ticket OK? . . . .Good. . . . .When does your train leave? . . . .OK. Is it alright if I pick you now and show you where I work and then take you to lunch? . . . . .Good. I'll be there in fifteen minutes."

The Linguistics Institute where Nicky works is located on the campus of Payap University and is staffed with people from all around the world. Seeking to preserve and develop ethnic languages which have no alphabet, Institute staffers spend hours and hours in tribal villages recording songs, stories and conversations. Linguists together with tribal people then analyze the languages and develop alphabets so that oral traditions can be preserved in writing and a literature developed.

The work of the Linguistics Institute is used heavily by missionaries so that they can communicate their faith with ethnic peoples and print Bibles. My son, who is an archaeologist, keeps reminding me that many anthropologists are critical of missionaries for undermining indigenous cultures. I know that in some cases this has been true, but the work of the Linguistics Institute reassured me that sometimes the work of Westerners in Thailand can actually help preserve indigenous cultures.

Nicky and I had lunch at a noodle shop near the train station, and I was back in my chair in the shade by 1:00 pm. Three more hours and I'd be on the train to Bangkok and on the last leg of my journey alone in Thailand.

While writing in my journal about the Linguistics Institute, I looked up and saw Sanit walking towards me. True to form, he was concerned about me and wanted to know if I needed anything. He sat in a chair next to me, and as we talked he put his hand on my arm. We talked for half an hour about the Nong Bua Sam Church, Nicky and M, his family, my health and the weather—all the while with his hand resting on my forearm.

Jiraporn &Sanit   *Nicky*
at Nong Bua Sam Church

In my experience, Thais are not demonstrative in showing affection. That, as I've already mentioned, is changing somewhat as the younger generation becomes more westernized and less traditional.

Sanit, however, is a traditional Thai in spirit even though he studied in the U.S., is very cosmopolitan, speaks English well and is technologically savvy, so the way he was expressing affection for me was another example of a Thai coming more than half way to me across the bridge between our two cultures.

He prayed for me, said "I'll see you next year," and walked away to his car, leaving me alone in the open air seating area with my luggage.

As they had done in the past, porters helped me find the car in which I belonged and helped lift my two bags, heavy with books and presents for people back home, aboard.

Secure in my little compartment and with no decisions to make for thirteen hours, I began to process what the day had given me. "What a difference a day makes," I thought as the train slowly wound its way through the mountains southeast of Chiang Mai. Gratitude had replaced irritation. Instead of judging Thai society to function worse than American society, I now felt like it worked better.

I have gotten somewhat used to my emotions alternating between positive and negative when I'm in Thailand or with the Thais in my church back home. Like the train I was riding on, for awhile we'd be slowly climbing up a grade and half an hour later we'd be flying downhill. One minute I'd be grinding my teeth and the next minute I'd be thinking, "How blessed am I to be here!"

Maintaining a measure of equanimity when living and working among Thai people has required that I acquire a fair amount of perspective and patience. I realized that Buddhadhasa would say it requires detachment, but I had to respectfully disagree with him as the train stopped at yet another town to pick up some passengers.

After pondering the day's events for a couple hours, I finally came up with the word I was looking for. The word was *humility*, not in the sense that I'm not worthy but in the sense that I figured out my place in the grand scheme of things. When I could see myself clearly and without apology as a disabled, male, Christian, highly educated American with all of the assets and deficits which that package includes, I am in a much better place to tolerate and even appreciate people who think, believe and behave differently than I do.

As I thought about this, a book entitled *The Big Sort* by Bill Bishop came to mind. In the book Bishop offers a ton of statistics showing that Americans are gradually choosing to move into communities of people who think like they do. In the town next to mine, for example, over 90% of the residents voted for Barack Obama in the 2008 election. Another example is that most churches in the U.S. boast that they are multicultural if just 5% of their members are of a different race. The tendency, Bishop argues, is toward the formation of homogeneous enclaves which partly explains the growing polarization in American society.

And I wondered if, contrary to America's self-image as a

melting pot, we aren't, perhaps unwittingly, moving into one of those historical periods in which people get tired of doing the hard work of dealing with diversity and feel like retreating into the comfort of sameness.

I know that was how I was feeling when I woke up that morning, and that's how I felt at the train station as I faced the prospect of being alone for six hours. I felt like I would rather be without anyone to talk to than to one more time do the difficult task of bridging another cross cultural chasm.

As I lay down on my convertible bed, pulled the curtain shut and tried to let the clickety clack of the train's wheels on the rails lull me to sleep, I got to thinking about why Nicky and Sanit keep doing the hard work of reaching out and welcoming me and others who are different. *Love* was he only conclusion I could come up with right before drifting off to sleep.

35

GRACE

The train pulled into the Hualamphong Station in Bangkok at 6:30 am. A porter waiting outside my car let me hop on his four wheeled cart along with my bags and chauffeured me out to the curb where I found a taxi which, after a 45 minute drive, dropped me off at the Luther Seminary in Thailand (LST) at 8:00 am.

The fourteen students at the small seminary were just finishing breakfast, so I was able to pull a chair up to one of the tables in the open air refectory and enjoy a big bowl of fish and rice soup. The president of the seminary, Dr. Banjob Kusawadee, showed me to my room on the second floor complete with a bed, bathroom, desk, air conditioner and a refrigerator—all for 500 baht ($17) a night.

It was good to see a familiar face after navigating the train and taxi rides on my own. Banjob and I have known each other for at least ten years through my visits to Thailand and his trips to Chicago. Having earned his Th.D. in Australia, his English is very good.

Ajahn Banjob

I had emailed him that I wanted to do research in the Lutheran Mission to Thailand Archives housed at LST, so he led me to the second floor office of the archives and introduced me to the young woman, nicknamed Sherrie, who was in charge. He apologized for having to leave me so quickly, and hurried down the stairs to yet another meeting. Talk about multitasking, Banjob is the seminary's president, teaches theology, is the pastor of three churches and soon after I returned home, he was elected Bishop of the Lutheran Church in Thailand.

The research I wanted to do was for a book I'm writing on the life of Pongsak Limthongviratn, my pastor back home at St. Paul Thai Lutheran Church. Pongsak had taught at and been the academic dean of the seminary before coming to the U.S. in 1989.

Sherrie found me a chair at a table and hurried out to bring me a glass of water and a cup of coffee. She then pulled out four huge binders from one of the bookcases, set them down on the table and asked if there was anything more she could do for me. And, yes, she was cute as a bug's ear.

I was a little afraid of opening the first binder. Everything had gone so well so far that day. What if the minutes were in Thai which I cannot read? The only reason I hoped that I could read the documents was because on past visits I had met some of the Norwegian and Finnish missionaries who still worked there and noticed that they all spoke impeccable English as well as fluent Thai as well as who knows how many other languages. Sure enough, the missionaries had decided to use today's *lingua franca*, English, for the minutes of their executive committee meetings.

I couldn't help thinking that Buddha would call my good fortune a result of my *karma* while Jesus would tell me it was another gift from a loving God. Before diving into the tedious work of examining hundreds and hundreds of pages of boring documents for entries having to do with Pongsak, I wondered if somehow the good I was experiencing could somehow be explained by both concepts simultaneously.

Around 2:00 I asked Sherrie if someone at LST could drive me over to the nearby Tesco Lotus big box store, so I could stock up my refrigerator to sustain me during the four days I'd be staying at the school. "No problem," she said as she picked up the phone. Within an hour and a half I had picked up fruit, soy milk and cookies and had them stored in my room.

I decided to eat dinner with the students in the refectory right down the stairs from my room. I enjoyed watching their horseplay and teasing. During dinner we played the same kind of game I had played in Nan, the game in which they used as many English words as they could and I tried to speak Thai, resulting in a lot of laughing. It was definitely *sanuk*.

After dinner I tried to stay up until 8:00. I had slept some on the train but not enough to carry me till 10:00. As I sat in air conditioned comfort on my bed, I marveled at how smoothly the day had gone for me, how all my prayers had been answered, so to speak. In fact, most of my forty day sojourn in Thailand, which was now winding down, had been filled with one good experience after another.

Many of my plans had not worked out the way I wanted, but like Mark said as we had reflected about travelling at the Riverside Bar in Lampang, often the times he had gotten lost had led to the best experiences.

Because I would be alone for much of the time, I had anticipated hours, even days of loneliness. Instead, the solitude had quieted my soul and allowed me to get more in touch with my self. I had imagined my vulnerability as a handicapped guy in a foreign country to create scary situations in which I would be taken advantage of. Instead, my limitations had most often become openings for people to care for me and create small, short term, intimate connections.

And here I was, sitting in a room in a Christian seminary right in the middle of six million Buddhists, trying figure out what it all meant. "Nothing happens by accident," I heard the Buddha insisting in my right ear. "Do good, receive good." And in my left ear I heard Jesus whispering, "The best things in life are free. Consider the lilies."

36

Banjob, Buddhadasa and Suffering

Banjob Kusawadee has always been religious. Even as a child, he took the inexorable law of karma seriously, trying to pile up as much merit as he could, so that he would be reincarnated into a better state in the next life and, in addition, could deposit some merit into his parents' spiritual bank accounts. His highest goal, however, was *nibbana* (nirvana), that state of nothingness or void, as Buddhadasa refers to it, which is the complete absence of suffering.

As Banjob tells the story, what tormented him was that he could never keep even the minimum five precepts: avoid killing, stealing, sexual misconduct, lying and alcohol/intoxicating drugs. It wasn't that he had gone out and killed anyone, but even as a boy he understood that the first precept had to do with inner states like the desire for revenge as well as outward actions. No amount of meditating could chase demons like greed and anger from his mind.

He therefore despaired of ever attaining the enlightenment which the Buddha had held up as the ultimate goal, because all of his efforts fell short of the mark. He confided this spiritual turmoil to his uncle, a Buddhist monk, and asked if it were humanly possible to become an *arahant*, i.e. one who has broken the wheel of birth and death. His uncle, an honest man, replied, "I'm not sure."

What struck him about the Christian preaching, which he heard during this time of spiritual struggle, was that the solution to the problem of living is a gift from God rather than a human achievement. That message turned his religious world view inside out. Using the metaphor I frequently find myself using, it gave him a lens through which he would see life's most profound issues very differently than he had as a Buddhist.

He was baptized as a teenager, entered what was called at the time the Lutheran Institute of Theological Education (L.I.T.E.), was ordained, and at the time of my visit was the President of the seminary from which he had graduated over twenty years before.

While talking with him during my four day stay at Luther Seminary in Thailand (LITE's new name) he gave me a copy of his doctoral thesis, *Holy Suffering*. I immediately took the book to my room and started reading, because his thesis seemed to be the perfect dialog partner for Buddhadasa Bhikkhu's *Heartwood of the Bodhi Tree*.

Sure enough. I started reading chapter one, turned the page and there read a quote from Buddhadasa. Banjob was familiar with the famous monk's thought. I read on, preparing for the attainment of a little enlightenment of my own.

I soon realized that Banjob and Buddhadasa—at least some of what Buddhasa had written--seemed to agree on one major point, that the two religions are very, very different. Banjob wrote, "Thai Buddhists are somewhat naïve in that they are inclined to believe that every religion is good and has the same purpose and goal. . . ." (*Holy Suffering*, p. 17)

And Buddhadasa had declared,

We can see the truth of this point [a discussion of the concept *ayatana*] taking a look at other religions. Other religions do not have the term *attavadupaddana* [clinging to the words "I" and "mine"] . . .because they teach a self to be grasped at and clung to. Because they do not regard such grasping as wrong, it becomes right; in fact it becomes the goal of that religion or sect. They teach the attainment of Self. In Buddhism, however, attachment to self is specified

as a defilement, as foolishness
and delusion. (*Heartwood*, p. 50)

As I read on, Banjob talked about suffering as a major issue in life, i.e. a problem that followers of Jesus try to mitigate if not remove completely. One thing which distinguishes Christianity from Buddhism, he said, is that a particular kind of suffering is also declared to be the solution. Suffering is a symptom of separation (detachment!) from God (whose name is *I AM*), and Jesus' suffering and death on the cross was God's solution to the problem of humanity's chronic willingness to become attached to gods who cannot come through with their promise to give life. In other words, God revealed an ultimate attachment to humans by dying for them, so that they would respond by reattaching themselves to God above all else.

Banjob put into words the reaction of many Buddhists to this idea of a suffering God, a reaction I had heard before many times.

If there is a God, he must be a cruel one or a
weak one, a suffering and stupid one, because he
does not know how to create a perfect world
or how to eradicate suffering....It is ridiculous
to ask help from the God who degraded himself to take the
form of a person who suffered and died on the cross....
If God could not deliver himself from suffering, how
can he extend his help to those who request it from him?
(*Holy Suffering*, p. 174)

In fact, I heard one Buddhist say in reference to some of the biblical statements about God yearning for and being passionate about his sheep who had gone astray that God needed to do some Buddhist meditation and try to attain a cool heart.

I set Banjob's thesis down to grab a Coca Cola Lite (what Thais call Diet Coke) from my little refrigerator. During my little break, I thought back to my encounter in the train station with Bhikkhu Buddha Dhatu, the good natured monk who had told me that all religions are the same. His heart was in a good place, I decided, but he was for some reason glossing over the glaring, profound differences.

Banjob clearly thought the two religions were different when he took the potentially isolating step of becoming a Christian in a country which is 95% Buddhist. Phra Peter Pannapadipo was of the same opinion when he went the other direction, leaving home, family and possessions in England to become a Buddhist monk in Thailand.

Phra Peter decided in middle age that Buddhism was "an alternative and more worthwhile way of living" than the nominal Christianity in which he had grown up. (*Phra Farang, an English Monk in Thailand*, p. 3) He added that the truth of a religious system can't be discerned by reading a book about it—what I would call being a *religious tourist*. "It's something," he declared, "which can only be understood experientially." (p. 147)

Trying to sort all this out made me think of book I had read in 1998 entitled *Salvations, Truth and Difference in Religion*, in which Mark Heim insisted that those who practice religion in its "thickest," most committed way will inevitably be exclusivist, i.e. they will consider their path to be the most profound when it comes to ultimate truth. "Religious traditions are simply, descriptively exclusivist," he wrote. "To know one is not to know the others. Each is a 'one and only...'" (p. 5)

Heim also argued that the different religions are trying to save people from different problems, i.e. not only are they different paths but the paths lead to different destinations. The whole Buddhist agenda, for example, is designed to liberate its adherents from suffering. That's why Buddhist meditation is so popular in the U.S. as a means for reducing stress. It works.

In contrast, Martin Luther King, Jr didn't do Buddhist meditation before a protest march. He sang gospel hymns with the marchers which empowered them to suffer without retaliation in pursuit of a just cause. His goal was not to escape suffering but to create justice.

I started to feel like I better understood Bill Yoder's statement that the Buddhists had converted him to Christianity. He was, in a way, complimenting the monks with whom he was dialoging. Just as athletes tend to perform best when competing against runners who are their equals, so faith can be tested and confirmed when it bumps up against another world view which is firmly grounded in a society.

I had suffered my share of losses in my 63 years of living—two marriages ending in divorce, the premature deterioration of my health and the subsequent loss of the work to which I had been called, the closing of my congregation, the deaths of my father and mother. In all of that loss, I could empathize with the Buddha's statement that nothing lasts, that everything is impermanent.

I could empathize but not agree with his response, because in the midst of the losses and the pain they produced, I experienced a constant equanimity, which my faith told me was God's loving presence. I couldn't prove that to my agnostic friend back home or to the Buddhist monks I met along the way and certainly not to the angry, anti-religion, Norwegian fellow I had encountered in Nan.

Not only that, but I had experienced some suffering as a positive, healing force. Years ago the leaders of my divorce recovery group kept on saying, "The only way out of pain is through it." They were right. That is why, I now realized, I had said to the man in Nan who admired my having a positive attitude in spite of my disability, "That may be, but it is only because I have done my grief work."

It's only been through suffering that I have matured to any degree. The demons inside, which kept me feeling like a little boy instead of a mature man, could only be quieted by facing them. That process has been frightening and painful, but the result has been liberating.

What's more, I've found that if I want to make any changes for what I perceive to be the common good--in my church, my condo building, my village—I'm going to suffer in the process. I never enjoy the pain, but the meaning I experience in working for something greater than myself is worth the struggle, whether I succeed or fail.

The spiritual bottom line for me is that I'm glad that the cruciform lens through which I view the world has taught me not only how to work through suffering instead of escaping it but also how "holy suffering," if you will, can paradoxically be used to reduce the net amount of suffering in the world.

I felt like I was getting somewhere with my puzzle pieces. A comprehensible picture was starting to form, until I remembered that in some places, Buddhadasa had said that all religions are the same. It bothered me that I couldn't figure out why he would say that Christianity and Buddhism are very different in one book and then contend that all religions are the same in another.

37

Pongsak

I went to the Lutheran Mission to Thailand archives four days in a row. Part of my motivation was that the room was air conditioned and the fixings for coffee were right down the hall.

But a bigger part was that it felt good to be working again.

My five weeks of wandering around Thailand had certainly not been a vacation. My spirit had been willing but my disabled, 63 year old flesh coupled with my significantly flawed psyche and my inability to speak Thai well often made me feel weak as I tested myself by being alone in Thailand. It was tiring work. I never had trouble falling asleep at the end of each day.

The work I had done during my first 35 days alone had been a different kind of work than the writing I do to supplement my income from disability. Writing is also hard work, and it makes me feel tired at the end of the day but also blessed. The blessing is that, as a writer, I get to use my God given abilities to make my little contribution to the common good. It also makes me feel grown up, like I know what I'm doing in at least one part of my life.

Writing mainly human interest stories for two local newspapers back in the Chicago area, I interview teachers and clergy and politicians and merchants—people enjoying success and people grieving the loss of a loved one, a business or an election--and simply tell their stories in a one or two thousand words.

Nothing I wrote ever changed the world. What mattered was that I was not only earning money to pay my bills, but I was part of that huge, amorphous team which is trying to make the world a better place. It's like the disciples when Jesus fed the 5000. It was Jesus who did the miracle, but those twelve guys got to hand out the bread and fish. They got to be part of the miracle, not because of any virtuous talent on their part, but because they had chosen to follow the right master.

It was good to get back to work again.

My research involved scanning hundreds of pages of Mission to Thailand Executive Committee meeting minutes looking for references to Pongsak Limthongviratn, whose biography I'm writing. One reason I want to write his life story is because he is a living metaphor for how to respond to a shrinking world and an increasingly multicultural society.

Pongsak has been a minority within a minority his whole life. When he was living in Thailand he was part of the ethnic Chinese minority there (10-15% of the population) and a Christian (>1%). When he and his wife Monta arrived in the U.S. in 1989, he became part of the Asian minority in both the nation and his church, the Evangelical Lutheran Church in America (ELCA).

On the one hand, he has responded to his minority status by building bridges to the dominant society. He speaks English very well in addition to being fluent in Mandarin and of course Thai. In order to get his Th.D. in systematic theology, he had to pass language tests in Greek, Hebrew and German. In his job in the Commission for Multicultural Ministry in the ELCA, he has learned to interact effectively with blacks, whites, Hispanics, Native Americans and all kinds of Asians. He owns a home in a suburb of Chicago, raised his two sons there and has learned to eat pizza.

On the other hand, part of his mission in life is to be an advocate and at times a fierce defender of the well being of his tiny minority group, the Thai Christians. Sadly, it hasn't been Buddhists in Thailand or Americans in general with whom he has had the most conflict. The tension has been mostly within the Lutheran church—with Norwegian and Finnish missionaries in the Lutheran Mission to Thailand and with the bureaucratic power structure in the ELCA.

The conflicts have usually been about money which means the issue has really been about power. When he would argue for Thai Christians making the decisions about the form and future of the church in Thailand, the missionaries would get their way and impose their ideas, because they had the money. Likewise, when he would advocate for Asians in America having control over how they do church in this country, he would be opposed by American bureaucrats who said they knew how to do things the right way and would threaten to withhold funding if they didn't get their way.

In a very real sense, Pongsak has been a foreigner wherever he has lived. He has tried to adapt respectfully to the dominant culture as long as doing so did not undermine his core identity or the identity and integrity of his small minority group. But whenever he sensed that his vulnerable constituency was being threatened by power elites, he would transform from an adapter to a fighter. He would fight fairly according to the rules, but he wouldn't hesitate to speak what he considered to be the truth to power.

I admire Pongsak very much, so much in fact that I look to him as a role model on how to lean into this increasingly diverse society in which we live. First, Pongsak knows who he is. He has clearly defined what he believes in and how those beliefs direct the way he lives. Second, because his core beliefs include love—not just of the neighbor but of the enemy as well—he bends over backwards to try to adapt to cultural and personality differences.

But third, bending over backwards to get along with people does not, for him, include letting people push him or his vulnerable group around. Fourth, when he fights, it's always in a defensive mode and according to the principles he believes in.

That's how all of my heroes—Dr. King, Dietrich Bonhoeffer, Oscar Romero, Desmond Tutu—lived. All four of these saints could be accurately labeled as conservatives in some ways and as liberals in others. All four transcended the kind of polarized partisan bickering so prevalent today in the U.S. They were radicals in the sense that they went to the *root* of what a meaningful, purpose filled life is all about.

It's interesting. Pongsak and I have worked closely together since 1992 and confer with each other several times a week. A few people in the ELCA admire our relationship and hold it up as a model of how people from a dominant culture can work respectfully with minorities. Yet, Pongsak and I are certainly not buddies. I'm not even sure the word *friends* describes our relationship. What we are, I have decided, is *brothers in Christ*.

That was a significant epiphany for me as I worked away in the air conditioned archives at a Lutheran seminary in the middle of a mainly Buddhist metropolis. Whereas the *Sangha* (the community of 200,000 Buddhist monks) is united by a common paradoxical goal, i.e. each individual monk independently pursuing his own attempt to detach from everything and everyone, Pongsak and I are united by our common attachment to One we both believe will save us. . .even if we must suffer at times on our path to freedom.

And that got me to thinking again about how the kingdom of God which Jesus talked about so much is like a foreign country, a "place" to which people from "this world" will feel strangely attracted to and at the same time will feel uncomfortable and insecure in.

I wondered where my allegiance really did lie. Do I feel more comfortable in "this world" or when I am on the road walking with Jesus' disciples? Was my ability to adapt to different cultures more like that of a chameleon, going along to get along without knowing whom I was following?

I have no doubt that Pongsak—like Bonhoeffer, King and Romero—would be willing to die for the One to whom he had surrendered his life. Would I be willing to make the same stand or was I trying to hedge my spiritual bets by trying to keep one foot in the boat of this world and the other on the dock of the kingdom of God?

38

Asian Lutheran International Conference

A man from the Luther Seminary in Thailand gave me a ride to the Bangkok Institute of Theology where I was to meet Pongsak and hitch a ride to Pattaya where I would spend my last day "alone" in Thailand with 150 Asian Lutherans from all over Asia and the Asian diaspora in the U.S.

As I waited for Pongsak at BIT, I said hello to many friends: Jenjira who had been my intern back in my congregation in 2004 and was now a professor at BIT, Surasak a professor who had picked me from the airport on my first visit to Thailand in 1994 and Nantiya, a BIT professor whom I had also met on my first trip. I had slept and eaten and worshiped at BIT so many times over the last 17 years that it felt similar to the Nong Bua Sam Church, a little bit like home.

The man who drove the car Pongsak had rented was an older seminary student named Saichon Kuhawan. His English was very good, so I was able to join in on parts of the conversation between him and Pongsak as we made the two hour drive from Bangkok to the resort town of Pattaya on the Gulf of Thailand where the sixth Asian Lutheran International Conference was being held.

Just like at BIT, I felt quite at home at the conference. I was able to say hello to many old Asian friends. On top of that, since the Asians at the conference spoke ten or more different languages, all the plenary sessions and worship services used English. I knew most of the opening worship service by heart, because it came straight out of the hymnal I had been using for 25 years.

It felt good to be on more familiar ground, to not feel so out of my element even though I was half way around the world from home, to feel at least a little bit like I knew what I was doing.

The comfort I felt with these somewhat familiar surroundings made me wonder if I was regressing, if so much time feeling like a learner had affected me negatively, so that all I wanted to do was retreat into a safe homogeneity.

While I was pondering all of this, I thought of Derek Petersen, a kid I had worked with in the senior high youth group while I was an intern in 1978 in Moose Lake, MN. Moose Lake was extremely homogeneous, very Scandinavian and very Lutheran. So where did Derek choose to study after high school but St. Olaf College which was more of the same.

After 20 years of not seeing each other, I met up with Derek in Juneau, AK while I was travelling along Alaska's Inside Passage. Derek was working as a lobbyist in Juneau for Alaska's public schools. As part of his work he had visited schools north of the Arctic Circle, had harrowing experiences with bush pilots, and shared meals with Inuits and Athabascans. As a lobbyist he worked with politicians, representatives from oil companies, tree huggers and native people.

When I remarked that relating to Inuits who lived on the Bering Sea was a big stretch from the parochial environment in which he had spent the first 21 years of his life, he nodded in agreement but added, "I think that growing up in that way is what frees me to relate comfortably with so many different kinds of people."

I've thought a lot about what Derek said since we had our conversation. I think what he meant was that his family, church and community had given him a clear sense of who he was.

My friend Derek had been given an identity which, perhaps

counter-intuitively, had made him so secure that he was not threatened by people from different cultures. He felt no need to be defensive or to convert them or to try to be like them. He was content with being himself and letting the people with whom he worked be themselves.

And, thinking about Derek made me recall a conversation with a friend back home named Karl Reko who had been a missionary forty years ago in Papua New Guinea. Reflecting back on his experience which included a lot of mistakes, he told me, "Your ability to be a good missionary will correspond directly to how long you can stand to be a baby. You're there to learn, learn, learn before you try to give them the gifts you have to offer."

I think Derek would add, "In order to tolerate always being a learner in a different culture, you have to know who you are and be secure in your identity."

Senex, a character in Madeline L'Engle's *A Wind In The Door* declared, "It is only when we are fully rooted that we are really able to move." (p. 190)

The more time I spent with my fellow Lutherans, the more I realized that my attitude towards Buddhism was changing. Throughout my time alone in Thailand I kept on having these imaginary conversations between the Buddha and Jesus in my head. What would Buddha say? What would Jesus say? The reason I had been doing this, I decided, was that I felt I needed to work down to the question of ultimate truth. In that regard, one had to be right and the other wrong.

That way of framing my encounter with Buddhism, I concluded, was due to the baggage I had inherited from the Enlightenment which I still carried around. Truth, Enlightenment thinkers had declared, must always be determined by reason and empirical observation. If you make a truth claim, they would argue, you had better be ready to prove it is true with facts and logical reasoning.

But what if ultimate truth is more relational that rational?

What if truth has more to do with whom you love than with what you know?

Another of L'Engle's characters says, "With my intellect I see cause for nothing but pessimism and even despair. But I can't settle for what my intellect tells me. That's not all of it. . . .And you and I have good enough minds to know how very limited and finite they really are. The naked intellect is an extraordinarily inaccurate instrument."(p. 87)

During the opening service for the conference, I received communion for the first time in almost two months. As often happens, I felt, at least temporarily, more connected to God after receiving. And it struck me that it wasn't a rational enlightenment that I had received but rather a relational connection.

I remembered that the Hebrew word translated as *to know* can mean to know a fact, as in I know that Springfield is the capital of Illinois. Or, it can mean to be intimate with another person, as in I know my son and daughter. To say I know Ben and Bekah well in no way implies that I have them figured out. They remain very much a mystery to me. What it does mean is that I am blessed with a strong, close relationship with them.

The result of all of this pondering was that my need to prove who was right—Buddha or Jesus—evaporated, because receiving communion reminded me that I *knew* whom I loved and who loved me. And being grounded--at least for a little while--in that love made me open--at least temporarily—to receive whatever gifts the Buddha had to give me.

What I was experiencing, I'm pretty sure, wasn't relativism or syncretism but the freedom to embrace diversity which being loved gives to people.

The upshot of all of this seems, paradoxically, to be that if people want to cross cultural boundaries in mutually respectful ways, they need to create and nurture well defined, healthy personal boundaries and a secure identity for themselves first.

Richard Rohr in *Falling Upward* argued that the first spiritual task in life is to build a strong identity or what he calls *a container.* He quotes the Dalai Lama as saying, "Learn and obey the rules very well, so you will know how to break them properly."(xiii)

"So we need boundaries, identity, safety, and some degree of order and consistency to get started personally and culturally," Rohr wrote. "We also need to feel 'special'; we need our 'narcissistic fix.' By that I mean, we all need some successes, response and positive feedback early in life. . . . You have to first have an ego structure to then let go of it and move beyond it."(pp. 3-5)

Before I left Chicago for my forty days alone in Thailand, I explained part of what I wanted to do by telling my friends, "When I'm alone in Thailand, my only travelling companions will be my self (sic) and God. I'm not sure if I'll be able to get along with either one."

I got to know both of them better in the solitude I had experienced as a visitor in a foreign land. Now I was ready to get to know them better through the familiar places and people back home.

39

SAVING THE WORST FOR LAST

I always feel anxious before catching a plane. I worry about forgetting my passport, getting there on time, making it through security. . . .even somehow getting on the wrong plane. I have nightmares about that.

So, it was a relief that the limo—a Lincoln Town Car—was waiting for me outside the hotel lobby at 4:30 a.m. and made what I thought would be a two hour drive in an hour and fifteen minutes. I had been through Suvarnabhumi Airport several times, so I knew where the United Airlines counter was. After checking my bags and getting my seat assignment, I was told to wait in a few minutes for a wheelchair to arrive.

Everything was going smoothly. While I waited for the wheelchair, I had time to eat the box breakfast the hotel had made up for me. Everything was going according to my schedule.

The first time I'd ever walked a labyrinth—it was at a convent along the Mississippi River—what struck me the most was that just at the point where it felt like I would reach the goal, the center, the path turned 180 degrees and headed in the opposite direction.

The wheelchair arrived and the driver took me to the expedited line for handicapped people like me. I knew the drill and had my passport ready. The Royal Thai immigration person checked it over, frowned and in pretty good English politely told me that I'd overstayed my visa.

"Some technicality," I thought as why wheelchair driver took me in the direction the immigration guy was pointing. "This will take just a minute to clear up."

The woman at the desk wasn't smiling. "Must have been brought up outside Thailand," I figured.

The sour puss looked at my passport and announced that I had overstayed my visa by 30 days. "You must pay 15,000 baht," she told me. I did a quick calculation--$600.

"But I had received a sixty day extended visa from the Thai consulate in Chicago," I protested.

"Yes, but when you entered Cambodia on Dec. 11, that voided your original visa. When you reentered Thailand, you were required to get a new visa."

"But, but no one told me," I lamented to myself. I can't remember if I prayed or not. Regardless, God knew what I was going through, but this time I wasn't miraculously bailed out—deus ex machine style—by Nicky or Sanit or some kind stranger.

Frugal—my friends use the word *cheap*—by nature, I'm not sure whether I was more upset about losing that much money, not having the guy at the border give me a heads up or the possibility of not getting to my plane on time.

I looked at the stern Thai official with my most helpless look and sighed. No response other than pointing to where I could exchange lots of dollars for Thai baht. My chauffeur wheeled me to the currency exchange. I handed my Forest Park National Bank debit card to the nice lady at the counter, who asked "how much" to which I replied "15,000 baht." She swiped the card and frowned. "Would not accept."

I clearly remember that at that point, I did consciously ask God to help me out of this. I also tried to detach enough from my panic to think clearly. The Buddha had taught me something that stuck. I had one other option. I handed the nice lady my Visa card—no pun intended—and prayed that it would work.

She swiped the card. I waited. She smiled. "OK," she said and handed me the biggest wad of Thai baht I had ever handled.

I heaved a sigh of relief that this turned out to not be the end of the world after all. I would pay the fine, get to my plane on time and get back home safely. . .that is if the plane didn't crash in the middle of the Pacific Ocean and me winding up alone on a deserted island like Tom Hanks in *Castaway*. It's hard to be detached and stay positive when you've just lost $600.

The plane took off on time. Circumstances were returning to normal, but not my internal equilibrium. "See what I mean?" said the Buddha sitting on my shoulder. "You get attached to things, and you suffer, because everything is impermanent."

Since the flight from Bangkok to Tokyo is five hours and then the flight from Narita Airport to O'Hare is another eleven, I had plenty of time to reflect on the meaning of the depression I was feeling.

It didn't take me long to come to a conclusion. The Buddha was right. I was clinging too tightly not only to my money but also to life going the way I wanted it to. But Jesus was right, too, and in a more profound way, at least in my view of things. I did get through the crisis. I did have this sense that I had been taken care of—not in the way I preferred, of course—and the grieving process wouldn't take too long. I began to feel better.

40

THE LONG JOURNEY HOME

As it often happens with me, it's only months or years later that a light goes on and I feel like I have figured out what happened "back when I was alone in Thailand" or anywhere else.

I continued to read Buddhadasa Bikku, and with the help of a PhD thesis entitled *A study of the dialogue between Christianity and Theravada Buddhism in Thailand* by the Rev. Dr. Bantoon Boon-Itt, I was able to figure out why Buddhasa was able to say that Buddhism and Christianity are the same. He was transposing Christian doctrine into Buddhist teaching.

The most striking example was argument that the Christian idea of *God* was the same as the Buddhist concept of *dhamma* or Buddha's teaching. "Dhamma is the same as that which is called God," he wrote. "Described in this way, God is the same thing as that which is called Dhamma in Buddhism." (*No Religion*, 1969, p. 227)

In the same book he wrote, "Whatever religious movement one may follow, if one holds tightly to one's master (for example, Jesus or the Buddha), then whatever else may be laid out before him, he remains attached to that master. He never comes to the point of going beyond, which is the point taught by that very master." (213-214)

Again, he writes, "Being bound in the prison of the good, attached to it and advancing to the highest good, to supreme goodness, supreme goodness will become the supreme prison, If it is like this, God himself will become the supreme prison." (184-185)

What Buddhadasa was arguing is that all religions are the same only if what they believe can be repackaged in Buddhist theological terms. God, therefore, can't be a "self" with whom a believer can have a relationship, because clinging to the idea of *I, me and mine* is the very delusion from which a Buddhist is trying to detach.

I again had the fantasy that Buddhadasa was like Cinderella's step sisters trying to force their Buddhist feet into Christian glass slippers, a venture which always ends up as a bad fit. And I had to conclude that what was motivating all of his declarations that Buddhism and Christianity are the same was that the good, well intentioned Bhikkhu—along with famous Buddhists like Thich Nat Han and the Dalai Lama—was really a romantic who wants so badly to love people of other religions and have everyone get along that he overlooks ways in which the object of his affection is profoundly different than he is.

Dr. Bantoon went even further and concluded that the famous monk was really an exclusivist or, at least, an inclusivist. "We can gauge the general perception of Christianity that was held by Buddhadasa," he wrote, "and conclude that he perceived Christianity to be a less developed religion."(p. 175)

Figuring that out made me feel better, not because I was vindicated in the sense that maybe I was right and the pluralists are wrong, but because I had my initial respect for the wise bhikkhu back. He had a core integrity which made him an honorable opponent against whom I could test my own faith.

After I returned home, I not only continued to read, but thoughts would pop into my mind from "out of nowhere." The intuition or insight or whatever you want to call it would come as I was showing my Thailand slides to friends or while I was in that liminal place between sleep and waking up or while reading a book.

For example, I was listening to an interview of a Catholic pro-choice activist named Frances Kissling during a broadcast of the *Civil Conversations Project* on NPR. She argued that the reason why pro-choice and pro-life people can't resolve their conflict is due to a reluctance of people on both sides to get vulnerable enough to 1) admit that they have some doubts about their own position and 2) acknowledge that the opposition might have some values that they can appreciate. Defensiveness, she said, is a symptom of insecurity. What is needed, she added, is an "enthusiasm for difference."

As I listened to Kissling, I recalled those evangelicals in the Buddha Park in Laos who prayed that God would rid the evil of Buddhism from that land. And I couldn't help wondering if they were insecure in their faith. I remembered that friend of mine who had said that evangelicals know they are right whereas Lutherans hope they are right, and I found myself being glad that I was a Lutheran.

I thought of Derek's contention that growing up in a tradition--which was homogeneous and at the same time didn't take itself too seriously--gave him the security that allowed him to have the very "enthusiasm for difference" that Kissling was saying was so necessary in our world. And I thought of Bill Yoder, who had lived and served in Thailand for nearly 40 years, who knew who he was and where he had come from, who loved the Thai people but resisted the temptation to try to be like them.

That same week I was interviewing Alex Kotlowitz for a newspaper article. Kotlowitz is a white guy who wrote a bestselling book called *There Are No Children Here* about what it is like to grow up as a black kid in Chicago's Henry Horner housing project. The occasion for the interview was a movie called the *Interrupters* which he and Steve James had made about CeaseFire in Chicago.

He was telling me that on the one hand he as a white guy was very conscious that he was an outsider on the west and south sides of Chicago, which caused him to be respectful and take the attitude of a learner. On the other hand, being an outsider allowed him to ask questions which the residents of those neighborhoods had stopped asking or lacked the perspective to ask.

Kotlowitz helped me understand why I am attracted to authors who in my mind write from the "margins" of the Christian church—people like Anne Lamott, Garrison Keillor, Annie Dillard and Frederick Buechner. It's why I enjoyed writing stories for my local newspaper about an Hasidic Rabbi, a Zen Buddhist Master and a Unitarian pastor. It's not that I have any desire to adopt their world views and belief systems. What they provide me with is a perspective from which I can ask questions about what I believe and how I live, questions which I and many of my co-religionists have been unable or unwilling to ask.

Going to Thailand so many times and being with a Thai congregation every Sunday has forced me to bump up against the fact that my own culture is far from perfect even though it was the one in which I am most comfortable.

*   *   *

And that, in a stream of consciousness fashion, led me to wonder again which culture I was most at home in, the kingdom of God or American society. I was forcefully reminded that my own religious tradition, the Lutheran church, was not the kingdom of God. It is clearly not the destination. It is a human construct, as Bill Yoder had reminded me, a vehicle. Hopefully, it is an adequate vehicle.

I decided that religions are like highways and denominations are like cars, an analogy I certainly did not invent. In the end, it's more important which highway I travel on than what kind of car I drive. To the east of Chicago, Interstates 80 and 90 share the same stretch of pavement through all of Indiana. If all of my driving was between Elkhart and Chesterton, I might assume that both roads lead to the same place.

As anyone, however, knows who has missed an exit on the interstate system, all roads do not lead to the same destination. If you take I90 to its western terminus, you wind up in Seattle. On I80 you'll arrive in San Francisco. Most adherents of Buddhism I've talked to, would protest that I don't understand them if I asserted that their road, like the Christian path, leads to heaven. They would correct me by explaining that their road leads to *nibbana,* no-thingness, no-self, void.

Which vehicle you drive, once you've chosen a road to travel, is another matter. Thai Buddhists have created a vehicle called *meditation* which can be driven on either 180 or 190, if you will. In some kinds of weather it performs as well or even better than the vehicle I know as liturgical worship. Thomas Merton, the Catholic monk, died in Bangkok while attending a conference on meditation in which he and Buddhists were trading tips on how to maintain and drive that particular spiritual vehicle.

Likewise, Christian denominations are like makes and models of different cars. Quakers understand silence better than anyone else. Mennonites are good at peacemaking. Liberal churches have an inside track on social concerns. Evangelicals understand the need for personal conversion.

In my home church, St. Paul Thai Lutheran Church, we have members who come from backgrounds as diverse as Seventh Day Adventist, Pentecostal, Southern Baptist and Presbyterian. There are even two Lutherans. The *unum* in the midst of all of that *pluribus* at St. Paul Thai Church is that at least we are driving on the same road in the same direction.

Most every Sunday, there are also Thai Buddhists sitting in the pews. They are welcomed and treated like celebrities. They come, because they want to check out an alternative route to the one they were raised to travel on. If their spiritual dissatisfaction was only with the vehicle they were raised to drive, they would try out Mahayana Buddhism or Zen. Same road, different vehicle.

That's as far as my analogy goes. It doesn't settle the question of ultimate truth. The Buddhists I've talked to say they want to get to Seattle. Devout Christians prefer San Francisco. That, of course, is where my analogy is inadequate. Both destinations are real cities on the West Coast, and if you arrived in one by mistake, it would still be possible to hop on a bus and get to where you wanted to be in a day or two.

Nibbana and heaven, that seems to be a different matter.

And I got to thinking that many of the people I know are not concerned very much with ultimate destinations. What matters to them is the journey. They don't seem to worry much about questions of ultimate truth. What matters is finding a way to feel spiritual. They are, it appears to me, more focused on vehicles which perform well than on where the road they are travelling ends.

That worries me, because I'll never forget hearing the story of two Germans who had been in Hitler's Nazi youth organization. They went on and on about how wonderful they felt—the torch light parades in stadiums filled with 60,000 people, the singing, the exhilaration of feeling like they were part of something bigger than themselves. And at the end of their story, the woman said, "But, he (Hitler) lied." And the man agreed, "Yes, he lied."

Regarding the concerns of the pluralists which are very real, I've decided that we don't have to pretend that all religions are the same when it comes to our ultimate destination, because from my experience with three religions—Judaism, Buddhism and Christianity—the rules of the road are almost identical. The Venn diagrams of the three ethical systems overlap each other close to 100%. Devout Muslims and Buddhists make great neighbors, especially if they occasionally share their cooking with me.

Seven months after returning home, I was reading a book entitled *Resident Aliens* in which Stanley Hauerwas and William Willimon argue that the Kingdom of God is a foreign country in relation to American culture and even the American church, that in God's kingdom not only will the values be different from the materialism, consumerism and individualism which mark American society but more than that, the Kingdom of God proposes a picture of reality which markedly changes how residents with that perspective view life in this world.

That different perspective changes reality, as it were. It's like the world is viewing life through the lenses in a microscope—there's the lens metaphor again--which allows it to observe a portion of reality invisible to the lenses in our eyes, parts of reality like an amoeba swimming around in pond water and nuances in fingerprints. The world's perspective has its place.

The problem with viewing life through a microscope, however, is that the viewer will never see the stars. The lenses won't permit that part of reality to be observed, and those who demand evidence, or at least experience, before they will "believe" something to be true, will decide that the star gazers' claims are implausible.

"OK," I thought, "that helps me understand why my agnostic friends or the Buddhist monks at *Wat Chedi Luang* have a hard time accepting my truth claims. They'll never see the stars I see until they are willing to look at the darkness of the night sky through a telescope." But the problem remains. Why do I have such a hard time seeing the stars, when I think that I'm using the right set of lenses?

From my point of view, of course, the lens through which I attempt to view ultimate reality enables me to see the stars more clearly than does Buddhism or the Enlightenment. But, we Christians are still "looking through a distorted glass dimly." To change the imagery, we might have papers that say we're residents of the Kingdom of God, but we behave and respond to the events of our lives like immigrants right off the boat.

In a paradoxical way I need the perspective of Buddhists and agnostics to help me see the limitations of my own lenses, narratives, myths and sensibilities. Allowing my self (sic) to be vulnerable to their questions has often been uncomfortable.

Ultimately, the purpose of authentic religion, however, is not to make me comfortable but to get me where I want to go. The grace filled paradox was that forty days alone in a foreign land forced me to learn more about my self and my home land than I did about Thailand and the people who called that country home.

My "home" isn't at 315 Marengo in Forest Park any more than it is in the Lutheran Church. I have been fairly comfortable in both places. So were the Israelites in Egypt. They, in fact, complained to Moses that they wanted to go back to the security of Egypt even though they were slaves there. The road to *The Promised Land* turned out to be rougher than they had fantasized. To paraphrase my divorce recovery group leaders, they wanted the way out of pain to skip over the pain. To use Erich Fromm's language, they wanted to "escape from freedom."

I had not been tested in the wilderness like the Israelites had for forty years or Jesus for forty days, but I had been tested. The question, it turned out, was not whether I had passed or failed the test but what I had learned from it. The test was a learning opportunity.

What I learned was that I liked my real self better than the self I sometimes pretended or strived to be; that God's way of doing things is a lot better than mine; and that the faith tradition in which I'm embedded is right where I want to be this side of heaven.

The irony, the paradox is that I have my time alone in Thailand and my encounter with Buddhism to thank for that gift.

+   +   +

Thailand Reading List

Below you'll find books I've read which are about or set in Thailand. In each category, I've listed them in order of how much I liked them. They are all in English, some translated and some were written in English. I bought almost all of the books below at a bookstore in Chiang Mai called Suriwong Book Center which has a good selection of books in English.

Memoir

**Karen Connelly, Touch the Dragon, Silkworm Books; also published as Dream of a Thousand Lives, Seal Press. A young Canadian woman spends a year in rural Thailand as an exchange student. Insightful and well written.

*Phra Peter Pannapadipo, Phra Farang, An English Monk in Thailand, Arrow Books. An English guy gets into Buddhism and becomes a monk in Thailand. Thai Buddhism is a syncretistic mix of a lot of things in addition to what Gautama taught. This book gives you a feel for what it's like in the every day lives of the monks and lay people.

Peter Jaggs, Blundering Around Isaan, Bangkok Book House. An English man winds up living in a remote rural village in Northeastern Thailand and tells stories about his experiences with shamans, Thai boxers, farmers and ordinary people who aren't sophisticated in a Western educated sense but know how to subsist on and coexist with the land and each other. Jaggs is a really good, self-effacing story teller.

Elayne Clift, Achan—A Year of Teaching in Thailand

Christopher Johnson, Siamese Dreams, Bangkok Book House. Another insightful memoir by a Westerner. Johnson is kind of an amoral guy who goes to Thailand, bumbles around, and grows to appreciate Thai culture and people. This is not spiritually inspiring but has tons of insights on Thailand.

Navarat, M.R. Nimitmongkol. A Victim of Two Political Purges. Silkworm Books. Navarat was himself imprisoned for participating in what some call a coup d'état and others call a revolution in Thailand in the early 1930s. It's part of the history of Thailand's still uncompleted journey to democracy. The only English thing I have found on that period but in my opinion he is pedantic and self-serving.

Jampee Tawylert, Wall Against the Wind, A Thai woman's true story, Heaven Lake Press. A story about Tawylert's childhood in rural Thailand in the 1970s. A window into traditional Thai culture in the family and village.

Carol Hollinger, Mai Pen Rai Means Never Mind, Asia Books.

Louise de Courval, Papaya Salad (make it spicy, please!) Fond memories of Thailand and Beyond, Post Books.

Ken Klein, Building a House in Thailand

Dr. Iain Corness, Farang

Travel Guides

Lonely Planet is the only guide I've ever used. It tends to be written for travelers on a budget like college students. I think it focuses more on "mom and pop" restaurants, etc. which I think are more interesting. Others in our groups have like several different guides.

Murder Mysteries

*Nick Wilgus, <u>Mindfulness and Murder</u>, Silkworm Books. Much like Tony Hillerman weaves Navajo culture into his murder mysteries, Wilgus includes insights—often wise—into Thai Buddhism and culture. A good read. The main character is a Buddhist monk, Father Ananda who used to be a cop. While he is trying to detach from life, he keeps getting involved in murder cases.

Nick Wilgus, <u>Garden of Hell</u>, Silkworm Books. Another in the Father Ananda series.
Nick Wilgus, <u>Garden of Evil</u>
Nick Wilgus, <u>Killer Karma</u>

Christopher G. Moore, <u>Asia Hand</u>, Heaven Lake Press. Shows the seamier side of Bangkok—crime, prostitution, drugs, poverty—survival of the fittest.

Colin Cotterill, <u>The Coroner's Lunch</u>. Soho. The first in a series of murder mysteries set in Communist Laos in the 1970s. A fun read. Gives some insight into life in the country just north of Thailand.

*John Burdett, <u>Thailand 8</u> 2004
        <u>Bangkok Tattoo</u>
        <u>Bankok Haunts</u>
        <u>The Godfather of Katmandu</u>

Novels

Khammaan Khonkhai, <u>The Teachers of Mad Dog Swamp</u>, Silkworm Books. A first year teacher gets assigned to a small rural village. Mixes rural life with a thread of big corporate corruption and destruction of the environment.

Botan (pseud. Supa Sirising), <u>Letters from Thailand</u>, Silkworm Books. Told through the eyes of a Chinese immigrant (Thailand is over 10% ethnic Chinese) who comes to Thailand following WWII and starts a business. Wonderful depiction of both ethnic and generational tensions in Thailand. Written in the form of letters to his mother back in China.

Jane Vejjajiva, <u>The Happiness of Kati</u>, Piggy Bank Press. The back of the book states:

A bestseller in Thailand, this pignant and beautifully written novel is the story of a 9 year old girl whose mother is suffering from ALS. Kati's spirited response to the challenges she faces and the evocative Thai setting make this poetic novel especially memorable.

Kukrit Pramoj, <u>Four Reigns</u>, Silkworm Books. An historical novel about a girl who lives through the reigns of four of Thailand's kings. You can learn a lot about Thailand history in the first half of the 20th Century and have a good read at the same time.

Kampoon Boontawee, <u>A Child of the Northeast</u>, Pouyzian Publisher. Another story of a child growing up in the very poor northeast part of Thailand known as Esarn. Charming. Terrible editing. Lots of spelling and grammatical mistakes but a good story.

John Hoskin, <u>Falcon at the Court of Siam</u>, Asia Books. An historical novel set in the 1600s that describes the arrival of Europeans and how they interacted with Thai culture and politics. The main character, Constantine Phaulkon, really did serve the king of "Siam" as a trusted advisor.

Alex Garland, <u>Beach </u>Navarat, M.R. Nimitmongkol. <u>The Dreams of an Idealist</u>. Silkworm Books. Kind of autobiographical fiction about the turmoil in Thailand in the early 1930s. Not great literature in my opinion.

Siburapha, <u>Behind the Painting</u>

Mischa Berlinski, <u>Fieldwork</u>, 2008

Rattawut Lapcharoensap, <u>Sightseeing</u>, 2005

Jerry Hopkins, <u>Thailand Confidential</u>, 2005
<u>Bangkok Babylon</u>

Alex Garland, <u>The Beach</u>, 1998

SP Somtow, <u>Jasmine Nights</u>, 1995
<u>Dragon's Fin Soup</u>

Tarmo Rajasaari, <u>Vapour Trails</u>

Pira Sudham, <u>The Force of Karma</u>, Shire Asia Publishers. Contrasts the lives of the rich and spoiled with the hard scrabble life of many rural Thais.

Neville Allen, <u>Saving Face</u>

SHORT STORY COLLECTIONS

Khamsing Srinawk, <u>The Politician and Other Stories</u>, Silkworm Books. Small snapshots into the struggles of the rural poor with a streak of social consciousness.

Christopher Moore, <u>Chairs</u>, Heaven Lake Press. Bangkok from a *farang* (foreigner) point of view.

S. P. Somtow, <u>Dragon's Fin Soup and Other Modern Siamese Fables</u>, Asia Books.

Siburapha, <u>Behind the Painting and Other Stories</u>, Silkworm Books. Well written short stories. The first story is 100 pages and is a love story. The last three are kind of pro-poor people pieces and anti-rich.

NON-FICTION

*Thich Nhat Hanh, <u>Being Peace</u>, Parallax Press. A contemporary interpretation of Buddhism.

*Swearer, Donald, <u>The Buddhist World of Southeast Asia</u>, Silkworm Books. Picture a Thai Buddhist taking a course on Jesus at the University and then come to the US and visiting real churches. That's what this book does. It goes beyond the basics you learned in college and describes the real practice of Buddhism in Thailand.

Steven Asma, <u>Buddhism For Dummies.</u> A great summary of Buddhist teaching with helpful illustrations.

Segaller, Denis. <u>Thai Ways</u>. Silkworm Books. Segaller is a farang (foreigner) who has lived in Thailand for decades and is married to a Thai. The book is a collection of over 50 newspaper stories written to help English speakers understand everything from the Thai festival called Songkran in which everyone gets everyone else soaking wet to figuring out how to tell time by the Thai system.

William Klausner, <u>Thai Culture in Transition</u>, The Siam Society. The author has lived in Thailand for over 50 years, has been a consultant to the Thai government as well as NGOs and has taught at both Thammasat and Chulalongkorn Universities. He is an insightful observer of contemporary Thai society.

David Wyatt, <u>Thailand, A Short History</u>, Silkworm Books. This is not light reading, but if what you want is just the facts from prehistoric times to the turn of the century, this is a good volume.

George Bradley McFarland, <u>Historical Sketch of Protestant Missions in Siam 1828-1928</u>, White Lotus Press. If you want to get a taste of how the old style missionaries thought, this is a great book. If it seems old fashioned, it's because it was first published in 1928.

Patricia Symonds, <u>Calling in the Soul</u> about Hmong people.

Pira Sudham, <u>People of Esarn</u>
             <u>The Force of Karma</u>

Anthony Walker, ed., <u>Mvuh Hpa Mi Hpa, Creating Heaven, Creating Earth</u>

BUDDHIST

P.A. Payutto, <u>Buddhist Solutions</u>
W. Vajiramedhi, <u>Looking Death in the Eye</u>
Bikhu Buddha Datu, <u>The Truth of the Messengers</u>
Acariya Thoon Khippapanyo, <u>Change Your View, Change Your Life</u>
*Buddhadasa Bikhu, <u>Why Were We Born?</u>
Banjob, <u>Holy Suffering</u> (Christian response to Buddhism view of suffering)